Installation view: *Andrea Büttner*, MMK Museum für Moderne Kunst, Zollamt, Frankfurt am Main, Germany, 2013

Installation view: *Andrea Büttner*, MMK Museum für Moderne Kunst, Zollamt, Frankfurt am Main, Germany, 2013

Installation view: *Andrea Büttner*, MMK Museum für Moderne Kunst, Zollamt, Frankfurt am Main, Germany, 2013

Installation view: *Andrea Büttner*, International Project Space, Birmingham, UK, 2012

Installation view: *Andrea Büttner*, International Project Space, Birmingham, UK, 2012

Installation view: *Documenta 13*, Neue Galerie, Kassel, Germany, 2012

Installation view: *Documenta 13*, Neue Galerie, Kassel, Germany, 2012

Installation view: *Documenta 13*, Neue Galerie, Kassel, Germany, 2012

Installation view: *Documenta 13*, Queen's Palace, Kabul, Afg

Installation view: *Moos/Moss*, Hollybush Gardens, London, UK, 2012

Installation view: *Moos/Moss*, Hollybush Gardens, London, UK, 2012

Installation view: *Brannon, Büttner, Kierulf, Kierulf, Kilpper*, Bergen Kunsthall, Bergen, Norway, 2012

Installation view: *Brannon, Büttner, Kierulf, Kierulf, Kilpper*, Bergen Kunsthall, Bergen, Norway, 2012

Installation view: *Three New Works*, Artpace, San Antonio, USA, 2011

Installation view: *The Poverty of Riches*, Collezione Maramotti, Reggio Emilia, Italy, 2011–2012

Installation view: *The Poverty of Riches*, Collezione Maramotti, Reggio Emilia, Italy, 2011–2012

Installation view: *Der Engel der Geschichte (The Angel of History) 1964–1981*, Hollybush Gardens, London, UK, 2010

Installation view: *Der Engel der Geschichte (The Angel of History),* 1981, Hollybush Gardens, London, UK, 2010

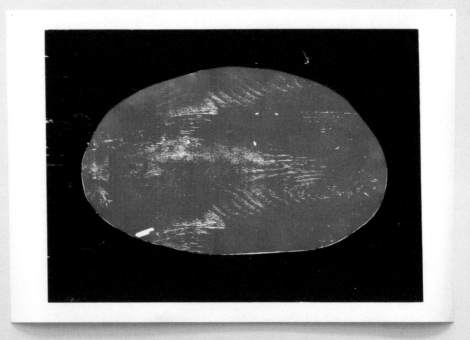

Installation view: *Unto this Last*, Raven Row, London, UK, 2010

THERESE
DE LISIEUX

LA PETITE SŒUR

les annáles
deSAINTE
THERESE DE
COLLECTION LA TRADI

»Ist nicht vor allem der ein Künstler,
dem es gelingt, uns das lieben zu lehren,
was ihm lieb ist?«
Hermann Hesse

Öffentliche Kunstsammlung
Kunstmuseum und Museum

Des Sitz der Gemeinde
Milieu für Schwellmuer
Lese Zeugnisse

des:

Installation view: *Vertiefen und nicht Erweitern*, SE8, London, UK, 2009

Installation view: *Nought to Sixty*, Institute of Contemporary Arts, London, UK, 2008

Installation view: *Soft Shields of Pleasure*, Den Frie Udstillingsbygning, Copenhagen, Denmark, 2008

Installation view: *Pensée Sauvage – on Freedom*, Frankfurter Kunstverein, Frankfurt am Main, Germany, 2007

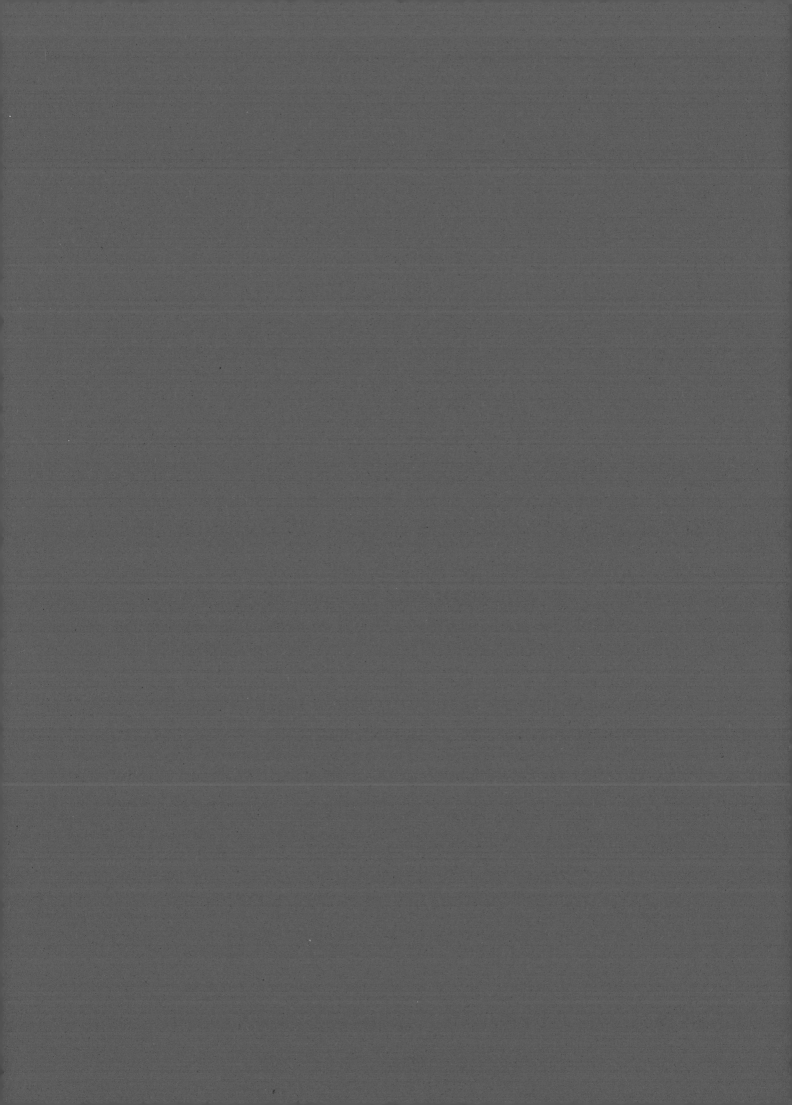

Andrea Büttner

MK Gallery, Milton Keynes, UK
MMK Museum für Moderne Kunst Frankfurt am Main, Germany
Koenig Books, London, UK

CONTENT

INHALT

L,M,A, 2006, screen print, 120 x 160 cm

The multi-faceted work of Andrea Büttner (born 1972 in Stuttgart) includes many techniques and subjects. The headlines feature woodcuts, video and reverse glass paintings in form, and judgement, vulnerability and embarrassment in content. But these interchangeable and interrelated features are all driven by a number of artistic strategies that emerged from a convent education, subsequent studies in art history and philosophy, and a doctorate on the subject of shame and art. These strategies include the adoption of a position of vulnerability (Büttner embraces a discourse of amateurism to contradict the expectation that art should look knowing, diligent or skilled), the interrogation of aesthetic and social uses of poverty (the artist constantly returns to iconography surrounding the legend of St. Francis where poverty is asserted as positive, revolutionary and beautiful), and art historical sampling to efface her own artistic persona (she frequently cites or refers to artists from Giotto to Warhol, via Sister Corita Kent, Dieter Roth and Valie Export). In relation to all of these approaches, Büttner also includes found material in her installations, proclamations of faith, and even sketches by her father, such as *Trinkende Tiere* (drinking animals) (2007) (pp. 267–73).

Perhaps all of these strategies are most clearly elucidated in an exhibition in 2010 called *Fallen lassen* (letting fall) (pp. 193–207). For this show, Büttner sought actions to express an 'affirmative attitude to falling', something akin to the German expression *Die Schultern fallen lassen* – to let your shoulders drop or 'fall down'. Instead of deliberately pouring or smashing things, she asked friends, artists, her dealer and a novelist to provide instructions on how to let something fall down in this manner. She then fulfilled

VORWORT

Das facettenreiche Werk von Andrea Büttner (1972 in Stuttgart geboren) umfasst zahlreiche Techniken und Sujets. Formal arbeitet sie mit Holzschnitt, Video und Hinterglasmalerei, inhaltlich geht es um Themen wie Wertungen, Verletzbarkeit und Verlegenheit. All diese wechselseitig eingesetzten und miteinander verbundenen Strategien sind wiederum im Kontext einer Klosterschulerziehung, dem Studium der Kunstgeschichte und Philosophie sowie einer Dissertation über Scham und Kunst situiert. Diese Strategien beziehen verschiedene Kriterien mit ein, hinter denen Büttner ihre eigene künstlerische Persona zurückstellt: eine Position der Verletzbarkeit (ihr Diskurs des Amateurs widersetzt sich der Erwartung, Kunst brauche Wissen, Sorgfalt und eine spezielle Technik), die Befragung der ästhetischen und sozialen Handhabung von Armut (durch ihren wiederholten Rückgriff auf die Ikonographie und die Legenden um den Heiligen Franziskus, in denen Armut als positiv, revolutionär und schön dargestellt wird) und kunsthistorisches Sampling (durch Zitate anderer Künstler, von Giotto über Sister Corita Kent, Dieter Roth und Valie Export bis zu Warhol). Darüber hinaus bezieht Büttner Fundstücke in ihre Installationen mit ein oder auch Skizzen ihres Vaters wie etwa *Trinkende Tiere* (2007) (S. 267–273).

Am besten lassen sich diese Strategien anhand ihrer Ausstellung *Fallenlassen* (S. 193–207) von 2010 erläutern. Dort suchte sie nach Aktionen, die eine „affirmative Haltung zum Fallen" ausdrücken, wie sie sich zum Beispiel in dem Ausdruck „Die Schultern fallen lassen" findet. Büttner verzichtete darauf, vorsätzlich etwas auszugießen oder zu zerschlagen, sondern bat Freunde, andere Künstler, ihre Galeristen und eine Schriftstellerin um entsprechen-

their instructions by, for example, placing a carrot and two pieces of coal on the floor and giving them the title *Memories of a Snowman*, in a passive process that positively embraces vulnerability, failure, damage, fragility, etc. In some respects, Büttner's work can be read as a series of behavioural studies with a par-ticular interest in ethical questions related to dignity or shame, self-consciousness or emancipation, value or poverty and the belief systems and conventions by which they are determined. With this complex, conceptual approach to making art, Andrea Büttner follows in the footsteps of such artists as Hanne Darboven, Martin Kippenberger and Rosemarie Trockel.

This book is the first substantial monograph on Büttner's practice and brings together images of her work from 2004 to 2013. It opens with a sequence of views from her most recent exhibition, at MMK Museum für Moderne Kunst, Zollamt in Frankfurt, which supplements the motif of the 'table' – reminiscent of refectories, canteens and soup kitchens – with works that expand on traditional concepts of 'poor' and 'rich'. The installation views in this book subsequently work backwards to earlier exhibitions, at Institute of Contemporary Arts, London, and Copenhagen's Den Frie, where the gallery walls were painted brown as high as she could reach. Other views include the presentation at *Documenta 13*, 2012, in Kassel with its focus on *Little Sisters: Lunapark Ostia*, 2012 (pp. 225–31), a video interview of nuns who manage an arcade in a small amusement park near Rome, as they visit attractions, ride on a roller coaster and speak about their work. Another shot shows Büttner's work at Documenta's off-site exhibition in Kabul, Afghanistan, where she showed a portfolio of twenty small woodcuts (pp. 275–87), which act as an index of symbols that appear across her practice, including a veiled figure, a donkey and a beggar.

de Anweisungen – trinken und Getränkedosen zertreten, eine Möhre und zwei Kohlestücke auf den Boden legen und mit dem Titel *Erinnerungen eines Schneemanns* versehen –, die sie schließlich in einem passiven Prozess befolgte, in dem sie Fallen, Scheitern, Schäden, Brüchigkeit usw. als positiv annahm. Büttners Werk kann in mancher Hinsicht als eine Reihe von Verhaltensstudien betrachtet werden, mit einem besonderen Interesse für ethische Fragen, die sich auf Würde und Scham, Schüchternheit und Emanzipation, Wert und Armut beziehen, aber auch auf die Glaubenssysteme und Konventionen, die diese Begriffe bestimmen. Mit ihrem komplexen, konzeptuellen Ansatz folgt Andrea Büttner Künstlern wie Hanne Darboven, Martin Kippenberger und Rosemarie Trockel.

Dieses Buch ist die erste größere Monographie über Büttners Arbeit und versammelt Abbildungen ihrer Werke von 2004 bis 2013. Am Anfang steht eine Bilderfolge ihrer jüngsten Ausstellung im MMK Museum für Moderne Kunst, Zollamt, in Frankfurt, die dem Motiv der „Tafel" als einer Erinnerung an Refektorien, Kantinen und Suppenküchen nachgeht und Arbeiten zeigt, die sich mit traditionellen Vorstellungen von „arm" und „reich" beschäftigen. Die Installationsansichten verbinden sich rückblickend mit früheren Ausstellungen am Institute of Contemporary Arts in London und im Den Frie in Kopenhagen, wo Büttner die Wände des Ausstellungsraums braun anmalte, so hoch ihre Arme reichten. Weitere Abbildungen zeigen ihre Präsentation bei der *Documenta 13* in Kassel, 2012, mit dem Blick auf *Little Sisters: Lunapark Ostia*, 2012 (S. 255–231), ein Video, in dem Nonnen, die in einem kleinen Vergnügungspark in der Nähe von Rom eine Spielbude betreiben, gemeinsam das bunte Treiben betrachten, mit der Geisterbahn fahren und über ihre Arbeit sprechen. Weiter gibt es ein Bild von Büttners

Adam and Eve, 2006, screen print, 120 × 160 cm

Running throughout this sequence of installation shots are discreet, structural elements, such as benches and corners, that form an important part of Büttner's practice. The benches are often planks of wood resting on grey plastic crates, with padded, woven back-rests, and offer a space of relaxation and contemplation for visitors. The corners, whether real or reproduced, are used partly to elicit feelings of embarrassment or remorse, with more than a nod to Kippenberger's penitent sculpture *Martin, Into the Corner, You Should Be Ashamed of Yourself* (1992).

Photographs of Büttner's works are loosely structured throughout this book according to medium and series, providing a general overview of her practice. This sequence begins with a series of screen prints (2006–2010) where the artist introduces a number of key motifs through a playful and personal take on devotional images, made with friends and family. The next sequence brings together woodcuts related to St. Francis of Assisi, including images of the tears that are said to have blinded him, the birds that he famously preached to, and the pebbles he begged for instead of bread (pp. 81–111). The images of cloth, tunics, even tents, equate shelter with clothing and recall the legend whereby St. Francis rejected his wealth by removing his fine clothes and returning them to his father. The reverse glass paintings are a series of glowing geometric abstracts painted on the back of glass that recall craft work, stained glass windows, and, like the woodcut grids further on, Modernists such as Kazimir Malevich. Some works in this series also include details from thirteenth-century Italian reliefs found on the tombstones of academics and professors in Bologna, depicting groups of students and scholars reading, listening and debating.

A sequence of unassuming photographs collected by the artist of moss growing over concrete paving, walls or bare soil (pp. 129–41)

Arbeit auf der Außenstelle der *Documenta 13* in Kabul, Afghanistan, wo sie ein Portfolio von 20 kleinen Holzschnitten zeigte (S. 275–287), das als Index der Bilder fungiert, die in ihrem Werk immer wieder auftauchen, darunter eine verschleierte Gestalt, ein Esel und ein Bettler.

Durch diese Installationsaufnahmen ziehen sich einzelne strukturelle Elemente wie Bänke und Raum-Ecken, die einen wichtigen Teil von Büttners Werk ausmachen. Bei den Bänken handelt es sich oft um Bretter auf grauen Plastikkisten mit gepolsterten Rückenlehnen, die den Besuchern einen Ort der Entspannung und Kontemplation bieten. Die Ecken, ob real im Raum oder künstlerisch hergestellt, werden eingesetzt, um Peinlichkeits- und Reuegefühle zu evozieren und spielen auf Kippenbergers Büßer-Skulptur *Martin, ab in die Ecke und schäm dich* (1992) an.

Die Abbildungen von Büttners Werken sind lose nach Medien und Serien geordnet und geben einen allgemeinen Überblick über ihre Arbeit. Am Anfang des Abbildungsteils steht eine Serie von Siebdrucken (2006–2010), in denen die Künstlerin durch eine spielerische, persönliche Sicht auf Andachtsbilder, die sie mit Freunden und ihrer Familie gemacht hat, eine Reihe von Schlüsselmotiven einführt. Die nächste Folge versammelt Holzschnitte zum Heiligen Franziskus von Assisi, darunter Bilder von Tränen, die ihn der Legende nach blind gemacht haben, der Vögel, denen er predigte, und den Stein, um den er statt Brot gebettelt hat (S. 81–111). Die Bilder von Stoff, Kutten und auch Zelten setzen Schutz mit Kleidung gleich und erinnern an die Legende, wonach Franziskus seinem Reichtum abschwor, indem er seine edlen Kleider ablegte und dem Vater zurückgab. Bei den Hinterglasmalereien handelt es sich um eine Serie leuchtender, abstrakter Bilder, die auf die Rückseite von Glas gemalt sind und Assoziationen zu Handwerk,

plays with a German expression that uses moss as a metaphor for money: 'Ohne Moos nichts los', or without moss you don't get anywhere. While also evoking Marcel Duchamp and Man Ray's *Dust Breeding* (1920), or the way Dieter Roth cultivated mould in his work, these images were first shown in the artist's London gallery at Hollybush Gardens. The subsequent *Fabric Paintings* might refer to the tunics of St. Francis, but also inevitably recall German artist Blinky Palermo's ready-made, department store fabrics stretched like canvases, although Büttner has replaced them with specific colours and fabrics related to workers' uniforms. The next sequence of woodcuts, which Büttner started making in the 1990s, was partly instigated by her interest in the German artist HAP Grieshaber (1909–1981). In the 1960s, Grieshaber taught this technique to a group of nuns, one of whom became Büttner's art teacher. The next photographs, taken from a magazine published by Grieshaber called *Engel der Behinderten* (Angel of the Disabled), show teenagers in psychiatric homes looking at his work. Through these images, which are as intense as Renaissance portraits, Büttner shows an uncomfortable tension between feelings of vulnerability and voyeurism. Started in 2008, some sculptural pieces – modest clay lumps kept moist or allowed to crack during exhibitions – have acted as surrogates for the artist's body. This sequence of images includes a rough 'dirty' diamond plopped on a Monobloc chair, a photograph of a cash machine smeared in faeces and a clay fountain, shaped like a pair of giant breasts discreetly spouting water. All these pieces are reminiscent of embarrassing, hidden, bodily attributes – the fluids, secretions and leaks, the wrinkles and cracks, – that are redolent of ageing and fatigue. Together, they present the interdependent and relative values ascribed to actions that are culturally unacceptable and conventional symbols of wealth and aspiration, such as money and diamonds.

Glasfenstern, aber auch, wie die Raster-Holschnitte an anderer Stelle an Modernisten wie Kasimir Malewitsch erinnern. Einige Arbeiten dieser Serie nehmen Details aus italienischen Reliefs des 13. Jahrhunderts auf, die Gruppen von Studenten und Professoren beim Lesen, Zuhören und Debattieren zeigen und von Grabsteinen von Professoren aus Bologna stammen.
Eine Sequenz unauffälliger Fotos von Moos auf Betonwegen, Wänden oder nacktem Boden, die die Künstlerin gesammelt hat (S. 129–141), spielt mit der metaphorischen Gleichsetzung von Moos und Geld: „Ohne Moos nichts los." Diese Bilder, die auch Marcel Duchamps und Man Rays *Dust Breeding* von 1920 oder die Schimmelkulturen im Werk von Dieter Roth evozieren, wurden erstmals in der Londoner Galerie der Künstlerin, Hollybush Gardens, gezeigt. Die darauf folgenden „Stoffbilder" beziehen sich möglicherweise wieder auf den Heiligen Franziskus, sie erinnern aber vor allem an die Arbeiten von Blinky Palermo, der handelsübliche Stoffe wie Leinwand auf Rahmen spannte; Büttner hingegen verwendet Farben und Stoffe von Arbeitsuniformen. Die folgenden Holzschnitte, mit denen sie in den 1990er Jahren begann, sind zum Teil von HAP Grieshaber (1909–1981) inspiriert. In den 1960er Jahren brachte Grieshaber diese Technik einer Gruppe von Nonnen bei, darunter auch der späteren Kunstlehrerin Büttners. Es folgen Fotos aus der von Grieshaber herausgegebenen Zeitschrift *Engel der Geschichte,* die Jugendliche aus zwei Behin-dertenheimen bei der Betrachtung seiner Werke zeigen. Mit diesen Bildern, deren Intensität an Renaissanceportraits erinnert, vermittelt Büttner eine unbehagliche Spannung zwischen Verletzbarkeit und Voyeurismus.
Seit 2008 dienen Skulpturen – ungebrannte Tonklumpen, die feucht gehalten wurden oder während der Ausstellung Risse bil-

Apron, 2007, screen print, 120 × 160 cm

The next sequence of images revolves around *Little Works* (2007), where the artist handed her camcorder to a Carmelite nun and asked her to film inside her cloistered convent in London (pp. 233–9). The result is a short film of nuns making objects or 'little works' in their free time, such as lavender bags and recycled candles, displaying what one of the nuns calls 'the richness of community'. The following photographs of white, plastic chairs were taken by Büttner on her travels across the world between 2010 and 2012 (pp. 249–57). These ubiquitous, stackable Monobloc chairs – replete with grid pattern and social and sociable potential – provide both an 'international community of chairs' and a synthetic equivalent of the proliferating moss project.

An important image towards the end of the book is of a woodcut depicting Roth and Kippenberger, two influential artists who made a virtue of self-abasement, in full debauchery mode, talking 'about their anxieties' (p. 303). This work shows Büttner's acute awareness of the potency of this attitude as an artistic strategy and her ability to channel similar sentiments within her own artistic voice. A couple of further images present views of installations with sound pieces in which Büttner reads from other artists' texts, including Sister Corita Kent and Roth. In Roth's case, Büttner singled out sections from his diaries expressing feelings of shame and embarrassment, but on a more conceptual level, by reading his words aloud, Büttner inserted herself as a medium between author and reader, toying with theories of production and reception; reading itself, of course, constitutes an act of production.

Actions like reading other people's writings, fulfilling instructions given by other people, citing thirteenth-century Italian reliefs, handing over a camera to a nun for *Little Sisters*, etc. are all ways of playing out Büttner's key strategies around value, vulnerability

deten – als Surrogat des Körpers der Künstlerin. Die Abbildungen zeigen einen braunen Rohdiamanten auf einem Monobloc-Stuhl, das Foto eines mit Fäkalien beschmierten Geldautomaten und einen Tonbrunnen, geformt wie ein Paar große Brüste, aus denen Wasser rinnt. Das alles erinnert an peinliche, verborgene körperliche Attribute – Flüssigkeiten, Sekrete und Lecks, Falten und Risse – und enthält Anspielungen an das Altern oder Müdigkeit. Die Skulpturen verweisen auf die Interdependenz und Relativität der Werte, die mit kulturell inakzeptablen Handlungsweisen und konventionellen Symbolen von Reichtum und Sehnsucht, zum Beispiel Geld und Diamanten, in Zusammenhang gebracht werden.

Weitere Abbildungen zeigen *Little Works* (2007), einen kurzen Film über Karmelitinnen, den eine Nonne in dem von außen unzugänglichen Teil ihres Klosters in London mit der Videokamera der Künstlerin aufgenommen hat (S. 233–239). Der Film zeigt, wie die Schwestern in ihrer Freizeit Objekte oder „kleine Werke" anfertigen, etwa Lavendelsäckchen und recycelte Kerzen, die in den Worten einer der Schwestern „den Reichtum von Gemeinschaft" darstellen. Es folgen Fotos von weißen Plastikstühlen, die Büttner auf ihren Reisen zwischen 2010 und 2012 aufgenommen hat (S. 249–257). Die allgegenwärtigen, stapelbaren Monobloc-Stühle mit ihrem Rastermuster und ihrem gesellschaftlichen und geselligen Potential stellen sowohl eine „internationale Gemeinschaft von Stühlen" als auch ein synthetisches Äquivalent zum wuchernden Moos-Projekt dar.

Ein wichtiges Bild gegen Ende des Buches zeigt einen Holzschnitt mit den beiden einflussreichen Künstlern Roth und Kippenberger, die die Selbsterniedrigung zur Tugend erhoben haben, in ihrer ausschweifenden Art und Weise „über ihre Ängste" sprechen (S. 303). Dieses Werk vermittelt Büttners genaues Gespür für die

Floating Figure, 2008, screen print, 120 × 160 cm

and visibility. Through these gestures, Büttner becomes like a medium concerned with displaying, showing, channelling and enabling, positions that are echoed in some of the final images such as Malin Ståhl (her gallerist) holding up a piece of clay (p. 323) for inspection and Sister Corita installing works in an exhibition (p. 325). Even the final image presents a ramp that literally enables access into a church, an allegorical tool that effectively offers a route to redemption and enlightenment (if not also to such counterparts as suppression and renunciation).

A number of texts run alongside these images, written by leading art writers who are also friends and associates of the artist. They provide in-depth and illuminating commentaries, reflections and interpretations of some of Büttner's work. Also included are the transcripts of talks on the subject of poverty held at a dinner in Büttner's exhibition at MMK in Frankfurt on 1 March 2013, and of *Corita Reading* (2006) and *Roth Reading* (2006) .

This artist's first comprehensive monograph has been devised and produced by many people, to all of whom we are deeply indebted. It has been developed to coincide with two exhibitions, one at MMK Museum für Moderne Kunst, Zollamt, in Frankfurt, skilfully organised by Bernd Reiss and Marijana Schneider, and the other at MK Gallery, Milton Keynes, excellently organised and delivered by Claire Corrin and Melanie Appleby. The publication itself is indebted to the expert management and organisational skill of Eva Huttenlauch and Claire Corrin and we are also extremely grateful to the authors for their revealing contributions and to the designers Quentin Walesch and Stefano Faoro for beautifully bringing all the disparate parts together. Thanks too are due to the artist's assistant Alanna Gedgaudas, who brought her precision and thoroughness

Wirksamkeit dieser Haltung als künstlerische Strategie, aber auch ihre Fähigkeit, ähnliche Empfindungen mit der eigenen künstlerischen Stimme zu artikulieren. Es folgen Ansichten von Installationen mit Klangarbeiten, in denen Büttner Texte anderer Künstler vorliest, darunter von Sister Corita Kent und Dieter Roth. Die von ihr gewählten Ausschnitte aus Roths Tagebüchern formulieren Gefühle von Scham und Verlegenheit. Auf konzeptueller Ebene positioniert sich Büttner durch ihr Vorlesen hier als Mittlerin zwischen Autor und Leser und spielt so mit Produktions- und Reproduktionstheorien, wobei natürlich das Lesen selbst einen Akt der Produktion bildet.

Ob sie nun fremde Texte vorliest, Anweisungen anderer ausführt, italienische Reliefs aus dem 13. Jahrhundert zitiert, für *Little Works* einer Nonne die Kamera überlässt – immer inszeniert Büttner Fragen nach Wert, Verletzbarkeit und Sichtbarkeit. Durch diese Gesten wird die Künstlerin zu einer Art Vermittlerin. Sie stellt aus, zeigt, kanalisiert und befähigt. In den letzten Abbildungen klingen diese Positionen noch einmal an, wenn ihre Galeristin Malin Ståhl ein Stück Ton zur Inspektion hochhält (S. 323) und Sister Corita Werke in einer Ausstellung installiert (S. 325). Das letzte Bild präsentiert eine Rampe, die im Wortsinne den Zugang zu einer Kirche ermöglicht, als allegorisches Vehikel auf dem effektiven Weg zu Erlösung und Aufklärung (wenn nicht dem Gegenteil: Verdrängung und Verzicht).

Zu diesen Abbildungen kommen Texte wichtiger Autoren, Freunde und Freundinnen sowie Kollegen und Kolleginnen der Künstlerin hinzu, die ihre Werke vertiefend und erhellend kommentieren, reflektieren und interpretieren; außerdem eine Mitschrift der Tischreden zum Thema „Armut", die anlässlich eines Abendessens in Büttners Ausstellung am 1. März 2013 im MMK Museum für

Parents in Church, 2006, screen print, 120 × 160 cm

to bear on all aspects of this endeavour, and to the unstinting commitment of the artist's gallerists Lisa Panting and Malin Ståhl at Hollybush Gardens, London.

This publication would not have been possible without the immense generosity of a few enlightened individuals and the artist would like to join us in particularly thanking Valeria and Gregorio Napoleone as well as Shane Akeroyd, Elisabetta Buonaiuto, André Gordts, Phillip Keir, Barry Rosen, Federico Santilli, Bina von Stauffenberg and those who wish to remain anonymous. The Goethe Institut London, and particularly Eva Schmitt and Maja Grafe, have also kindly offered their assistance. The exhibition supporters in Frankfurt include Kulturamt der Stadt Frankfurt, Freunde des MMK and Jürgen Ponto Foundation for the Support of Young Artists.

Finally, we would like to express our admiration and gratitude to the artist for her openness and generosity throughout this whole process, not only in preparation for this ambitious book but also in devising two simultaneous exhibitions of ever-increasing breadth and reach.

Susanne Gaensheimer, Director, MMK Museum für Moderne Kunst Frankfurt am Main, Germany
Anthony Spira, Director, MK Gallery, Milton Keynes, UK

Moderne Kunst, Zollamt, in Frankfurt gehalten wurden, sowie Ausschnitte der Arbeiten von Dieter Roth und Sister Corita Kent, denen die Transkripte von Büttners Klangarbeiten *Corita Reading* (2006) und *Roth Reading* (2006) entnommen sind.

An der Entwicklung und Produktion der ersten umfassenden Monographie über die Künstlerin waren sehr viele Menschen beteiligt, denen wir zu tiefem Dank verpflichtet sind. Sie erscheint parallel zu zwei Ausstellungen, einer im MMK in Frankfurt, organisiert von Bernd Reiss und Marijana Schneider, die andere in der MK Gallery, Milton Keynes, zusammengestellt von Claire Corrin und Melanie Appleby. Diese Publikation ist dem Sachverstand und Organisationstalent von Eva Huttenlauch und Claire Corrin geschuldet, und wir danken besonders auch den Autoren für ihre aufschlussreichen Beiträge und dem Graphikdesigner Quentin Walesch, der gemeinsam mit Stefano Faoro alle Inhalte so wunderbar zusammengebracht hat. Dank gilt ebenso der Assistentin der Künstlerin, Alanna Gedgaudas, die sich mit Präzision und Gründlichkeit aller Aspekte dieses Projekts angenommen hat, und der Unterstützung der Galeristinnen Lisa Panting und Malin Ståhl von Hollybush Gardens, London.

Dieses Buch hätte ohne die außergewöhnliche Großzügigkeit engagierter Menschen nicht erscheinen können. Unser Dank, dem sich die Künstlerin anschließt, gilt vor allem Valeria und Gregorio Napoleone, aber auch Shane Akeroyd, Elisabetta Buonaiuto, André Gordts, Phillip Keir, Barry Rosen, Federico Santilli, Bina von Stauffenberg und anderen, die ungenannt bleiben möchten. Auch das Goethe-Institut in London und dort insbesondere Eva Schmitt und Maja Grafe haben uns ihre freundliche Unterstützung angeboten. In Frankfurt wurde die Ausstellung vom Kulturamt der

Tears, 2010, woodcut, 120 × 180 cm

Stadt Frankfurt, den Freunden des MMK und der Jürgen Ponto-
Stiftung zur Förderung junger Künstler unterstützt.
Und schließlich möchten wir der Künstlerin danken, die den
ganzen Prozess mit so bewunderungswürdiger Offenheit und Großzügigkeit begleitet hat. Das gilt nicht nur für die Realisierung
dieses anspruchsvollen Buches, sondern auch für die Entwicklung
von zwei gleichzeitig stattfindenden und äußerst umfangreichen
Ausstellungen.

Susanne Gaensheimer, Direktorin, MMK Museum für Moderne
Kunst Frankfurt am Main
Anthony Spira, Direktor, MK Gallery, Milton Keynes

Bush, 2010, woodcut, 120 × 180 cm

Drinking Man, 2010, woodcut, diptych, 180 × 120 cm, each sheet

Vogelpredigt (sermon to the birds), 2010, woodcut, diptych, 180 × 120 cm, each sheet

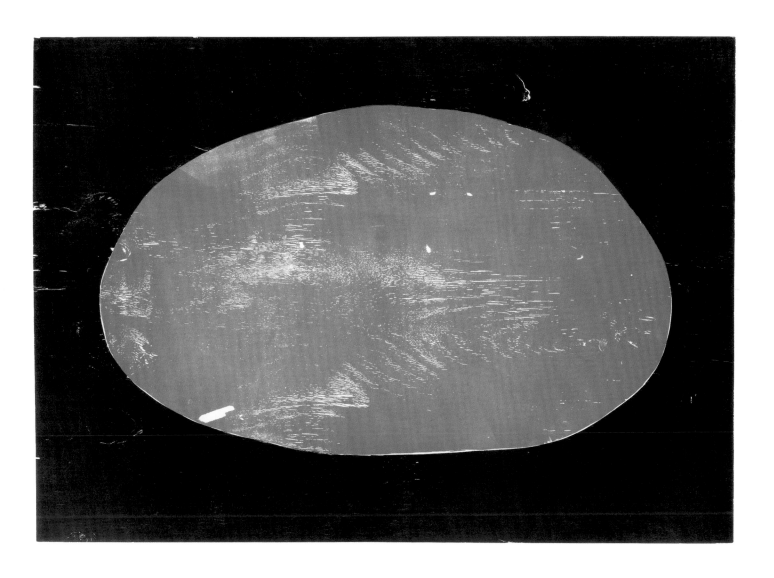

Table, 2010, woodcut, 147 × 142 cm

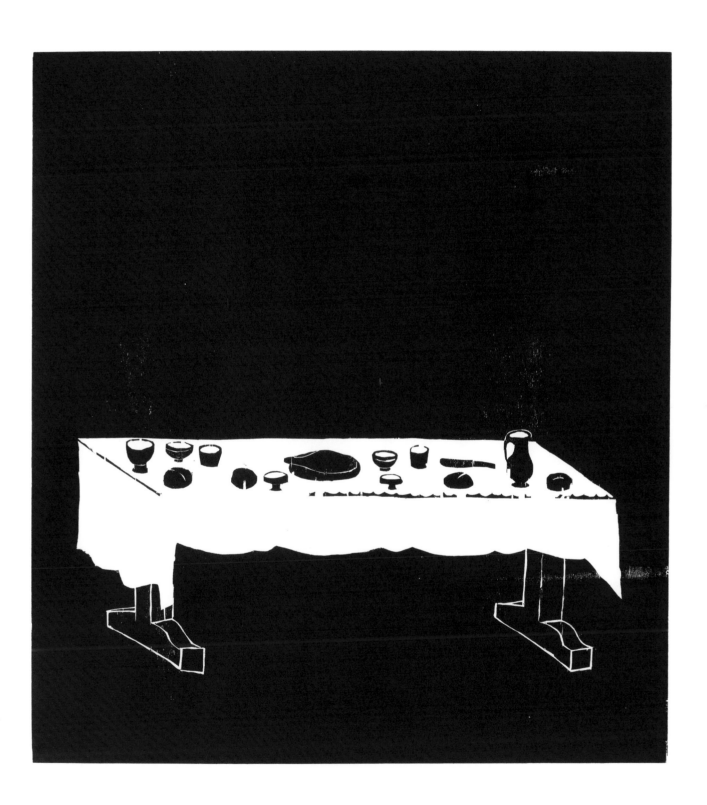

Man with fabric, 2010, woodcut, diptych, 118 × 178 cm, each sheet

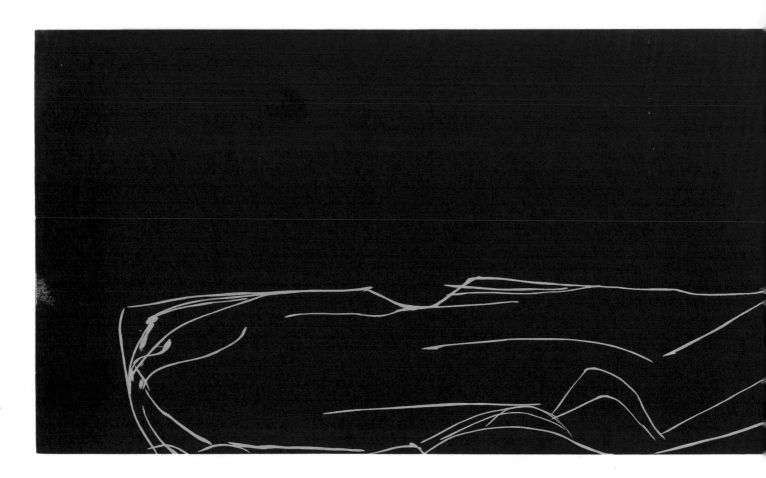

Tent (pink), 2010, woodcut, 130 × 218 cm

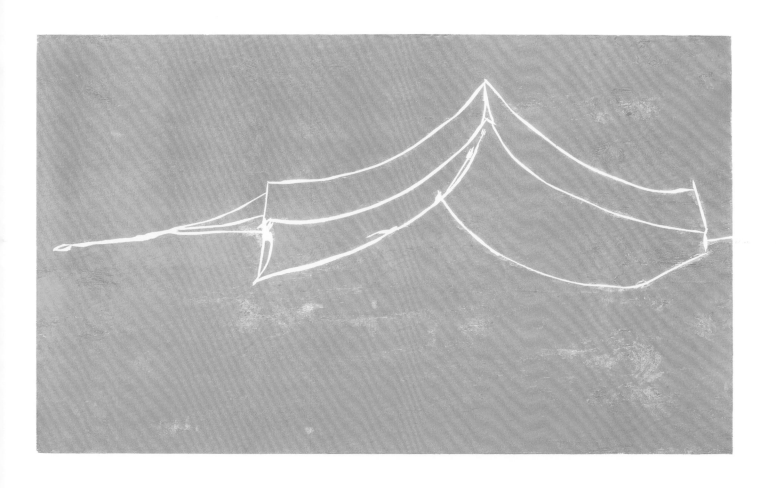

Tent (marquee), 2012, woodcut, diptych, 123 × 195 cm, each sheet

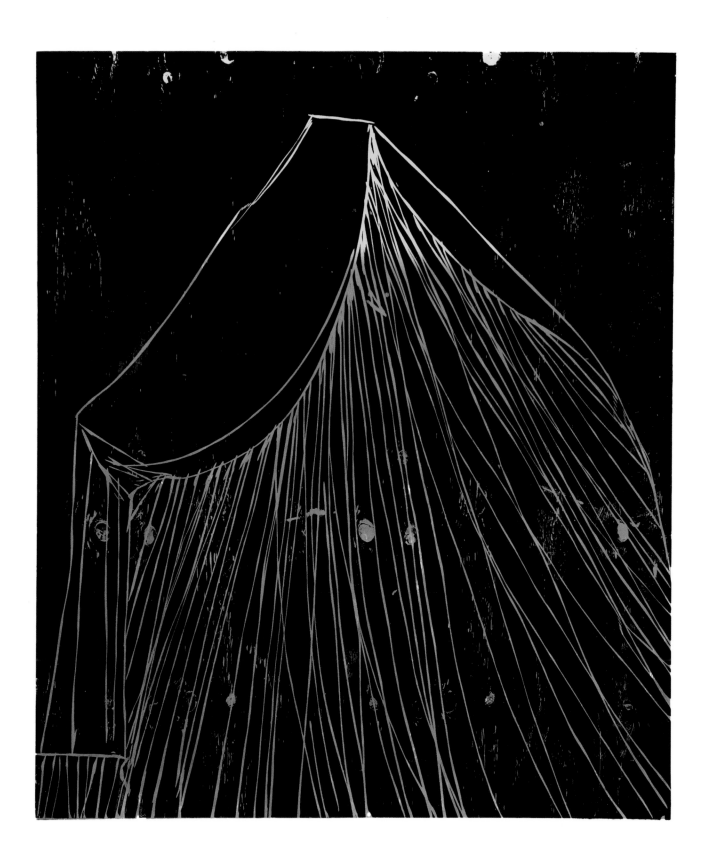

Tent (igloo), 2012, woodcut, 138 × 208 cm

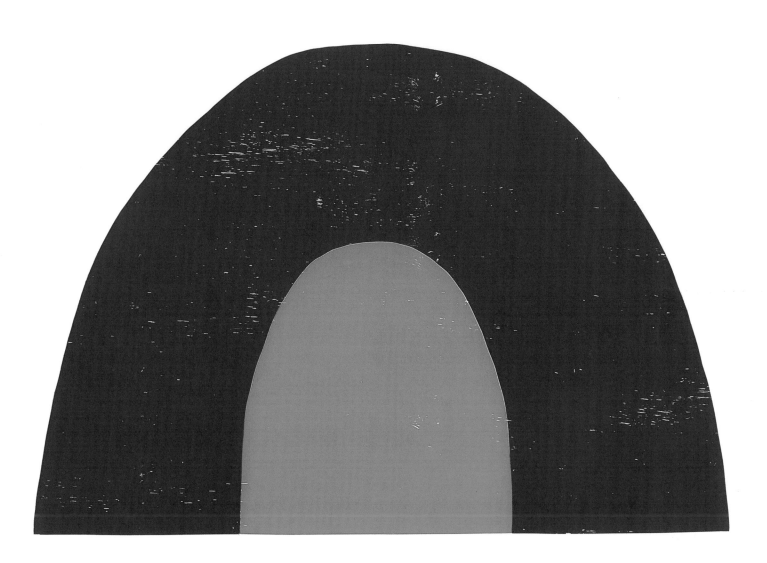

Predigendes Pferd (preaching horse), 2004, woodcut, 30 × 42 cm

Tiere Predigen dem Heiligen Franziskus (animals preaching to St. Francis),
2004, woodcut, 60 × 43 cm

Tent (two colours), 2012, woodcut, 142 × 232 cm

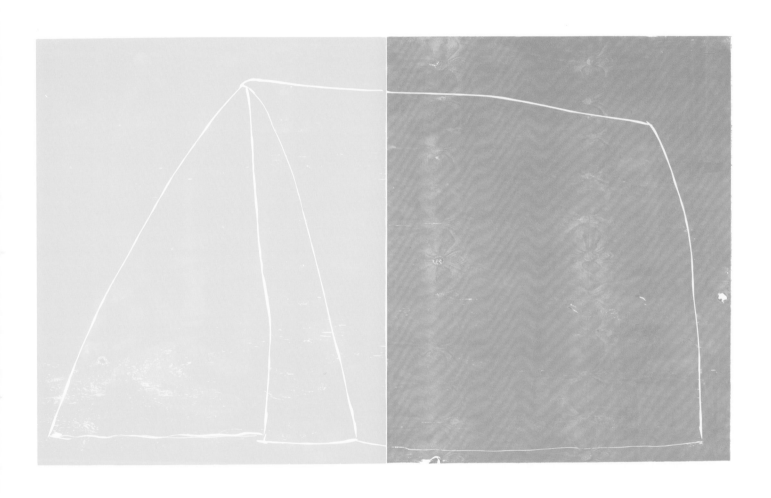

Untitled (three kings), 2012, woodcut, 130 x 214 cm

Braunes Grid, 2007, reverse glass painting, 27 × 33 × 0.2 cm

Untitled (smear of brown), 2011, reverse glass painting, 23 × 31 × 0.2 cm

Untitled (red, blue), 2011, reverse glass painting, 27 × 31 × 0.2 cm

Tre Fontane, 2010, reverse glass painting, diptych,
28 × 31 × 0.2 cm; 26 × 30 × 0.2 cm

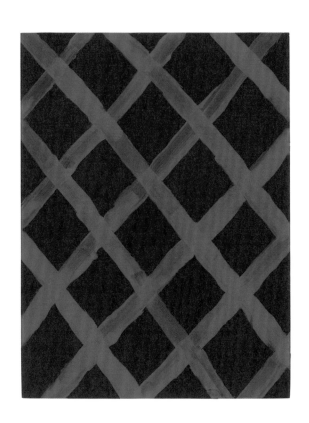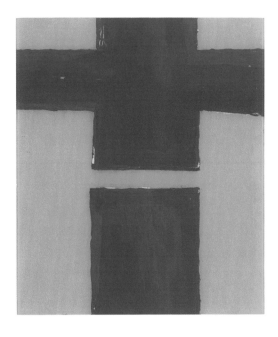

Potato, 2008, reverse glass painting, 25 × 25 × 0.2 cm

From Untitled (13th and 14th century gravestones depicting reading scholars
from Bologna University), 2012, reverse glass painting,
40 × 32 × 0.2 cm (green); 32,7 × 30.8 × 0.2 cm (red);
32 × 20.5 × 0.2 cm (yellow); 47 × 34 × 0.2 cm (black)

122
123

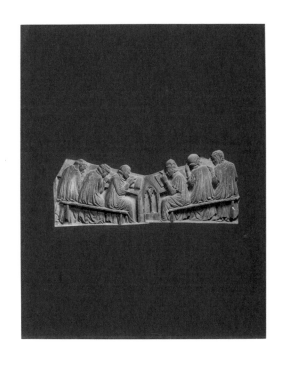

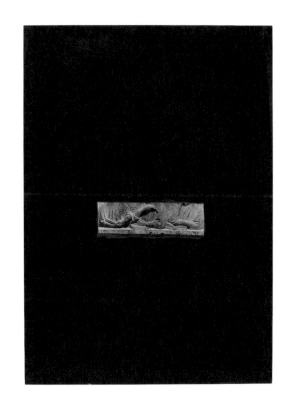

Untitled (grid – red, blue), 2012, reverse glass painting, 47 × 34 × 0.2 cm

Untitled, 2013, reverse glass painting, 19.3 × 24.5 × 0.2 cm

Cone, 2005, reverse glass painting, 19 × 19 × 0.2 cm

Holy Scheisse

When one sees death – not in film or on TV, but really sees it with one's own eyes – then death has a face: that of another human being, of a loved one. At the same time it is overwhelmingly abstract. It can be sublime and frightful, eternally sad, a release. To the weary old man and woman death may even be boring, because of its proximity over many years.

It is a different matter with processes of digestion that are out of the reach of our conscious being, and that produce dead, abject matter inside the human body. Shit makes human life shameful – yes, it even shames God. In his best-selling novel *The Unbearable Lightness of Being* (1984), Milan Kundera talks about the 'theodicy of shit': 'Shit is a more onerous theological problem than is evil. Since God gave man freedom, we can, if need be, accept the idea that He is not responsible for man's crimes. The responsibility for shit, however, rests entirely with Him, the creator of man.'[1] Or, perhaps it is the case that shit makes a mockery of everything because it makes death faceless?

At the rear end of value, Andrea Büttner's laconically titled installation *Three Little Works* (Artpace, San Antonio, 2011) included *Fountain* (2011), a clay fountain, shaped like a pair of giant breasts and discreetly spouting water from a hole at the top of each cone, a photo of a cash machine smeared with brown matter (*ATM*, 2011), and a white plastic chair with what appeared to be a semi-transparent pebble, but in fact was an uncut brown diamond, perched on top of it (*Diamantenstuhl* [diamond chair], 2011). There

---

Holy Scheiße

Wenn man den Tod sieht – nicht in Film oder Fernsehen, sondern real, mit eigenen Augen – dann hat er ein Gesicht: das eines anderen, geliebten Menschen. Gleichzeitig ist er überwältigend abstrakt. Er kann erhaben und schrecklich sein, ewig traurig, eine Befreiung oder, für müde alte Männer und Frauen, sogar langweilig, weil er ihnen viele Jahre so nahe war.

Anders ist es mit dem Verdauungsprozess, der außerhalb des Bewusstseins stattfindet und im Inneren des menschlichen Körpers einen toten, abstoßenden Stoff produziert. Die Scheiße beschämt das menschliche Leben – ja, sie beschämt sogar Gott. In seinem Romanbestseller *Die unerträgliche Leichtigkeit des Seins* (1984) spricht Milan Kundera von der „Theodizee der Scheiße": „Die Scheiße ist ein schwierigeres theologisches Problem als das Böse. Gott hat dem Menschen die Freiheit gegeben, und so kann man annehmen, dass er nicht für die Verbrechen der Menschheit verantwortlich ist. Doch die Verantwortung für die Scheiße trägt einzig und allein derjenige, der den Menschen geschaffen hat."[1] Vielleicht macht die Scheiße aber auch deshalb aus allem eine Farce, weil sie dem Tod das Gesicht nimmt?

Auf der Kehrseite des Werts verbindet Andrea Büttners lakonisch betitelte Installation *Three New Works* (Artpace, San Antonio, 2011) einen Brunnen aus Ton, geformt wie zwei gigantische Brüste, aus denen aus je einem Loch an der Spitze diskret Wasser rinnt (*Fountain*, 2011), das Foto eines mit braunem Material beschmierten Geldautomaten (*ATM*, 2011) und einen weißen Plastikstuhl, auf

was a fourth work too, namely a sound piece based on recordings of birds chirping in a chapel designed by James Turrell. Perhaps this was the reason why the title of the four works in the installation only acknowledged three: the last work was a kind of co-production between Büttner and another artist.

Comparable to how shit makes death faceless and abject, money is the substance that creates pernicious equivalence by consuming human minds and bodies. In Sigmund Freud's analysis of the relation between excrement and money, the former symbolizes the latter. According to Freudian symbolism, the appearance of human waste in a dream sequence makes the dreamer feel as if there are aspects of the self that are dirty, undesirable, or repulsive.

In psychoanalysis nothing is true except the exaggerations, Theodor Adorno wrote. Be that as it may, sometimes exaggeration is called for to see an antagonistic culture for what it is.[2] And so the installation's markers of compromised economic value – the shit-smeared cash machine, the diamond degraded by its immediate proximity to a lowly garden chair – draw up a moral battlefield between those forces that struggle for the conquest of our souls and societies: virtue and freedom, greed and ambition. The poverty of riches, the Franciscan way. Or, as per Henry Miller: the day that shit becomes worth something, the poor will be born without an arsehole.

As in other pieces, in *Three New Works* Büttner's practice enters in discussion with that of other artists, such as Andy Warhol, Sister Corita Kent, Martin Kippenberger, or art historical figures such as Giotto. In effect, her work forms already quite a crowd with a lively art historical discussion. *Diamantenstuhl* is in this way created in reference to Dieter Roth's fundamental notion that one makes an artwork by putting one thing on top of another.

---

dem ein halbdurchsichtiger Kieselstein liegt, bei dem es sich tatsächlich aber um einen braunen Rohdiamanten handelt (*Diamantenstuhl*, 2011). Es gibt auch noch einen vierten Teil, eine Klangarbeit auf der Basis einer Aufnahme von Vogelgezwitscher in einer von James Turrell entworfenen Kapelle, eine Art Koproduktion Büttners mit einem anderen Künstler. Das mag der Grund sein, dass der Titel dieser Installation nur drei der vier Teile würdigt.

So wie die Scheiße den Tod gesichtslos und abstoßend macht, so verzehrt das Geld Geist und Körper der Menschen und ist damit sein verderbliches Äquivalent. In Sigmund Freuds Analyse ist Geld das Symbol für die Ausscheidungen. Im Freudschen Symbolismus versteht der Träumende menschliche Ausscheidungen, die in einer Traumsequenz auftauchen, als Hinweis auf schmutzige, unerwünschte oder abstoßende Aspekte des Selbst.

„An der Psychoanalyse ist nichts wahr als ihre Übertreibungen", schrieb Adorno[2], aber manchmal braucht es die Übertreibung, um eine antagonistische Kultur als das zu sehen, was sie ist. Und so deuten die Marker des kompromittierten ökonomischen Werts in der Installation – der mit Scheiße beschmierte Geldautomat, der durch seine unmittelbare Nähe zu einem ordinären Gartenstuhl abgewertete Diamant – auf ein moralisches Schlachtfeld zwischen Kräften, die um unsere Seelen und unsere Gesellschaft kämpfen: Tugend und Freiheit, Gier und Ehrgeiz. „The Poverty of Riches" auf franziskanische Weise. Oder, mit William Burroughs: Sobald Scheiße etwas wert wird, werden die Armen ohne Arschloch geboren.

In *Three New Works* und anderen Arbeiten setzt sich Büttner mit anderen Künstlern auseinander, etwa Andy Warhol, Sister Corita Kent und Martin Kippenberger, aber auch mit Figuren

A review of the exhibition in which *Three New Works* was shown, largely consisted of a bemused and ultimately frustrated attempt at decoding Büttner's work. It concluded in this way: '... find Büttner's study in brown and white in the prestigious Artpace building, and so, in San Antonio. But how do you think her alignments of earthy tones with the scatological, with shame, would be received if the show were mounted instead at a Latino community center, such as the Guadalupe? How would the exhibit be read at the Esperanza Peace and Justice Center, at Centro Cultural Aztlan?'[3]

The criticisms levelled against her work are rather harsh, if also opaque. The critic suggests that race, and by extension class, are the work's blind spots, due to its supposed hierarchization of the colours brown and white. However, no artist who wished to maintain categories of hygiene would have exhibited a photo of a cash machine smeared in faeces. Nor would the diamond have been brown, and it wouldn't have sat on top of a plastic chair. It is not possible to establish a clean and unambiguous reading of the work based on colour, on any other formal or conceptual parameter for that matter.

One could reply to the Texan art critic that to be aesthetically literate is an overlooked precondition for comprehending social conflict. As demonstrated by Büttner, the brightest rooms are the secret domain of faeces. However, this wasn't Büttner's reaction. After having read the review she commented to me, 'Oh, they really didn't like my Artpace exhibition in San Antonio. I had to completely agree with them!' Why did Büttner mysteriously agree with the criticisms, when they were obviously wide off the mark?

In a very general sense, the hostile review affirms a limit to freedom that Kundera calls the theodicy of shit. As per Kundera's

der Kunstgeschichte wie Giotto. So gesehen, ist ihr Werk ganz schön bevölkert und führt eine lebhafte kunsthistorische Diskussion. *Diamantenstuhl* verweist denn auch auf Dieter Roths fundamentale Vorstellung, man schaffe ein Kunstwerk, indem man ein Ding auf ein anderes setze.

In einer Rezension der Ausstellung, in der *Three New Works* gezeigt wurde, versuchte Scott Andrews verwirrt und letztlich vergeblich, Büttners Werk zu dekodieren. Er schloss mit den Worten: „Sehen Sie Büttners Studie in Braun und Weiß im prestigeträchtigen Artpace-Bau und damit in San Antonio. Aber wie wäre die Verbindung von Erdfarben und dem Skatologischen mit der Scham in ihrer Installation wohl in einem Latino-Zentrum, etwa im Guadalupe, aufgenommen worden? Wie würde das Werk im Esperanza Peace and Justice Center, im Centro Cultural Aztlan verstanden?"[3]

Das ist eine scharfe, wenn auch unklare Kritik. Für den Kritiker sind Rasse und in der Erweiterung auch Klasse blinde Flecken des Werks, weil es die Farben Braun und Weiß angeblich hierarchisiert. Aber kein Künstler, der Kategorien der Hygiene bewahren wollte, würde das Foto eines mit Fäkalien beschmierten Geldautomaten zeigen oder einen braunen Diamanten auf einen Plastikstuhl setzen. Man kann auf der Basis der Farbe oder auch anderer formaler oder konzeptueller Parameter keine saubere, eindeutige Lesart des Werks etablieren.

Man könnte dem texanischen Kunstkritiker antworten, ästhetische Bildung sei eine häufig übersehene Voraussetzung für das Verständnis sozialer Konflikte. Die hellsten Räume sind, wie Büttner zeigt, geheime Domänen von Fäkalien. Büttners Reaktion war eine andere. Als sie die Kritik gelesen hatte, sagte sie: „Im Grunde mochten sie in San Antonio meine Artpace-Ausstellung nicht.

conviction that shit is a more onerous theological problem than evil, the Texan art critic develops an ideology critique of shit that insinuates that Büttner probably isn't evil, only a spoilt European artist, or some such thing. On his part, Kundera reduces the theodicy problem to a kinky philosophical mind game that is inconsequential to the non-believer. Contrary to this, Büttner's work implicates herself as an artist in a quite different way. In theory, for instance, she could – as a non-believer, if this is what she really is – make work on the subject of other religions than Christianity. When she chooses not to do so, her involvement in a Christian cultural sphere persists as a critical and self-reflexive moment in her work. Beyond this, Büttner demonstrates that faeces are a universal political marker. There are in fact historical precedents for this. In India, Gandhi instructed people to clean their own toilets. No one on the left had thought of that before – it used to be a low-caste job, reserved for the Dalit community.[4]

By positing shit as a political problem, established by the psychoanalytical correspondence between shit and money, Büttner calls up quite different limits to freedom: one acknowledges a radical simultaneity according to which all human beings live in a world bound together by a global marketplace, and in which people are placed and valorized in different ways according to the race, gender, class, community and sexual orientation they belong to. To make a couple of clay tit fountains with water coming out of them is thus a way of stating that you are no deeper than the shit you are in. One can only agree that it would have been interesting to see Büttner's show in a less reified context than the Artpace Foundation: just as she establishes parallels between the gallery and the monastery, in a sense her work is not – cannot be – disconnected from the local Latino community centre when it is shown in San Antonio, Texas.

Ich konnte ihnen nur vollkommen zustimmen!" Woher kam diese mysteriöse Bejahung einer doch völlig verfehlten Kritik?
Sehr allgemein gesehen, bestätigt die ablehnende Kritik eine Grenze der Freiheit, die Kundera als Theodizee der Scheiße bezeichnet. Wie Kundera, für den Scheiße ein schwierigeres theologisches Problem ist als das Böse, entwickelt auch der texanische Kunstkritiker eine Ideologiekritik der Scheiße, die unterstellt, dass Büttner zwar nicht böse, aber eine verwöhnte europäische Künstlerin sei oder etwas in der Art. Kundera seinerseits reduziert das Theodizee-Problem auf ein verdrehtes philosophisches Gedankenspiel, das für den Nichtgläubigen ohne Folgen bleibt. Dagegen bringt sich die Künstlerin Büttner auf ganz andere Weise in ihr Werk ein. Theoretisch könnte sie – als Ungläubige, wenn sie das wirklich ist – zum Beispiel über andere Religionen als das Christentum arbeiten; indem sie das nicht tut, bleibt ihr Engagement in einem christlichen Kulturraum ein kritisches und selbstreflexives Moment ihrer Arbeit. Darüber hinaus demonstriert sie, dass Fäkalien als politische Marker universell sind. Dafür gibt es tatsächlich historische Beispiele. So brachte in Indien Gandhi den Menschen bei, ihre Toiletten selbst zu reinigen. Kein Linker hatte vorher daran gedacht – es war eine Arbeit, die der untersten Kaste vorbehalten war, der Kaste der Dalit.[4]

Indem sie Scheiße als politisches, durch die psychoanalytische Entsprechung von Scheiße und Geld bestätigtes Problem postuliert, beschwört Büttner ganz andere Grenzen der Freiheit: die Akzeptanz einer radikalen Gleichzeitigkeit, die davon ausgeht, dass alle Menschen in einer Welt leben, zusammengehalten von einem globalen Markt, in der Personen je nach Rasse, Geschlecht, Klasse, Gemeinschaft und sexueller Orientierung unterschiedlich positioniert und bewertet werden. Wer einen Brunnen aus einem Paar

A garland of shame / Its thorn my only delight [5]

Next to its social dimension, Büttner's work is highly aware of itself as art. It creates a discussion about the meaning and problematics of the aesthetic through a high degree of attention paid to the cultural context of art production, for instance with regards to how political art looks, or what it is *supposed* to look like. This sensitivity gives her work its particular pulse, its push and pull between dynamics of involvement and critique, while it at the same time often positions itself at an uncomfortable distance from artistic concerns and media that are typically deemed contemporary. Büttner conceptualises shame as an aesthetic feeling, a paradigm for the reception and production of images and of art making. In her PhD she argues against the idea that we live in 'shameless times' and disproves the idea that shame has died. Confessional TV shows, celebrity culture, nudity in advertising, representations of sex, the blurring of the distinction between public and private are all taken to be indicative of a shamelessness of our time. However, the starting point of Büttner's research was the opposite observation: namely that shame is alive and well in today's visual culture. She writes:
'It might be empirically correct that we see more nakedness and sexuality on stages and screens, more public exposure of what was once deemed private – but we still feel shame on behalf of many things. The reasons for shame are varied and subject to change. Shame is still experienced – and it is key to an understanding of our behaviour in the realm of visual culture. A focus on sexuality in contemporary discourses on shame obstructs from the relevance this supposedly anachronistic and dead emotion holds in contemporary Western culture. It veils the fact that contemporary visual culture is still a "shame-culture" (...) My intuition was that

tönerner Titten macht, aus denen Wasser läuft, sagt damit, dass er nicht tiefer steht als die Scheiße, in der er steckt. Es wäre tatsächlich interessant, die Ausstellung in einem weniger verdinglichten Kontext als der Artpace Foundation zu sehen: So wie sie Parallelen zwischen der Galerie und dem Kloster gezogen hat, so ist ihr Werk, wenn es in San Antonio, Texas, gezeigt wird, vom lokalen Latino-Zentrum weder getrennt noch zu trennen.

A garland of shame / Its thorn my only delight [5]
(Eine Girlande der Scham / Ihr Dorn meine einzige Freude)
Neben seiner sozialen Dimension ist sich Büttner über den Kunstcharakter ihres Werks durchaus bewusst. Durch die starke Berücksichtigung des kulturellen Kontexts der Kunstproduktion – wie sieht etwa politische Kunst aus und wie „sollte" sie aussehen? – stößt es eine Diskussion über die Bedeutung und Problematik des Ästhetischen an. Diese Sensibilität verleiht ihrem Werk seinen besonderen Pulsschlag, sein Pendeln zwischen Engagement und Kritik, während es sich in einer unbehaglichen Distanz zu den typischerweise als zeitgenössisch geltenden künstlerischen Fragen und Medien positioniert.
Büttner konzeptualisiert Scham als ästhetisches Gefühl, als Paradigma für die Rezeption und Produktion von Bildern und von künstlerischer Arbeit. In ihrer Doktorarbeit wendet sie sich gegen die Behauptung, wir lebten in „schamlosen Zeiten", und weist nach, dass die Scham keineswegs tot ist. Fernseh-Beichtshows, Starkult, Nacktheit in der Werbung, Darstellung von Sex, die Verwischung der Grenzen zwischen dem Öffentlichen und dem Privaten gelten als Zeichen für die Schamlosigkeit unserer Zeit. Büttner ging in ihrer Forschung von der gegenteiligen Beobachtung aus: Scham ist in der heutigen visuellen Kultur lebendig:

it is precisely the realm of visual culture that is especially shame-prone. And accordingly, the more visually oriented a culture becomes the more shame-driven it might be (...) Shame is a necessary condition of visual culture: I will show you something, and you may look at it and make a judgement.'[6]

And she continues:

'Shame marks the threshold of visual representation and might at the same time be impossible to represent. Shame determines what we show or what we hide, what we expose and what we veil. Shame is intimately related to exhibiting, to the gesture of showing, to aesthetic judgement, and to the norms and conventions according to which we judge and move in the art world.'[7]

Büttner describes how in art school she felt ashamed about her art historical fascinations. She thought Vincent van Gogh's sunflowers were amazing, but was afraid to admit so because she knew that it would be considered *démodé* and uninformed. To make matters worse she worked with woodcut, which was 'the most uncool thing'.[8]

'Shame means that we resist what we desire,' Kundera writes, 'and feel ashamed that we desire what we resist.'[9]

But isn't Büttner's premeditated aesthetic embarrassment just a self-conscious kind of meta-cool? Ironically, such a stance wouldn't be so different from the second generation of institutional critique that was the gospel in the German art school system of the 1990s (and that shamed Büttner): like any brand of conceptualist art worth its salt, institutional critique needs an enemy, and therefore it has developed a parasitical relationship to the art institution – just like Büttner seems to do with the concept of coolness.

It is true that Büttner's work is a kind of counter-institutional critique – for instance, because she accepts the notion of an 'art world' in her writing, and fundamentally agrees with the sociological

---

„Es mag empirisch richtig sein, dass wir mehr Nacktheit und Sexualität auf Bühne und Leinwand sehen, mehr öffentliche Darstellung des einst Privaten – aber wir schämen uns dennoch für vieles. Die Gründe für Scham sind vielfältig und der Veränderung unterworfen. Scham wird immer noch erlebt – und ist der Schlüssel zu einem Verständnis unseres Verhaltens im Bereich der visuellen Kultur. Der Fokus auf Sexualität in den gegenwärtigen Diskursen über Scham lenkt von der Bedeutung dieses heute in der westlichen Kultur angeblich anachronistischen und toten Gefühls ab. Er verdeckt die Tatsache, dass die zeitgenössische visuelle Kultur weiterhin eine 'Schamkultur' ist. (...) Für mich schien aber gerade der Bereich der visuellen Kultur besonders anfällig für Scham. Und entsprechend beeinflusst die Scham eine Kultur besonders dann, wenn diese visuell orientiert ist. (...) Scham ist eine notwendige Bedingung der visuellen Kultur: Ich zeige dir etwas, und du kannst es betrachten und beurteilen."[6]

Und weiter: „Scham kennzeichnet die Schwelle der visuellen Darstellung, kann aber unter Umständen gleichzeitig unmöglich darzustellen sein. Scham bestimmt, was wir zeigen und was wir verbergen, was wir offenbaren und verschleiern. Scham ist eng mit dem Ausstellen verwandt, mit der Geste des Zeigens, dem ästhetischen Urteil und den Konventionen, nach denen wir urteilen und uns in der Kunstwelt bewegen."[7]

Büttner beschreibt, wie sie sich auf der Kunstakademie ihrer Begeisterung für die Kunstgeschichte schämte. Sie hielt Van Goghs Sonnenblumen für fantastisch, hatte aber Angst, es zuzugeben, weil sie wusste, dass es als „démodé" und naiv galt. Dass sie Holzschnitte machte, das „uncoolste überhaupt", machte die Sache nicht besser.[8] „Scham bedeutet", sagt Kundera, „daß wir uns gegen etwas wehren, was wir wollen, und darüber beschämt sind, daß wir wollen, wogegen wir uns wehren."[9]

Moos/Moss, 2010–2013, fabric painting and monitor with digital slide show, 200 × 116 cm

analysis of how value is bestowed upon the artwork by the field of art and visual culture. Witness her video piece *Little Works* (2007), in which English nuns are interviewed about their handicrafts, in monastery jargon called 'little works'. It is hard to not see the work as an allegory of the narcissistic projects of self-realization of the creative classes. In her work she turns shame into a performance, whose score is the strategic reading of the art world and whose stake is subjectivity, or what we could call 'the aesthetic self'. Strategic, because woodcut, for instance, is no longer considered a 1980s thing that male painters once produced, and therefore deemed unfashionable. It is not uncool any more. Büttner's is not quite a refusal to play the game (even if her work seems to ironically privilege a certain kind of passivity over innovation as a conventional artistic virtue), but an attempt at changing the stakes of the game by refusing to accept its normative values. In this way she keeps challenging exclusionary definitions of the political artwork, for instance by defying the taboo of the religious as a legitimate subject for contemporary art.

Moreover, her work has ultimately nothing of the moral priggishness of the less self-reflexive versions of institutional critique that believe themselves capable of denuding and touching power as such. As already mentioned, her work opens up to history and society at large, and to an analysis of subjectivation in visual culture, which gives her work an entirely different scope. Instead Büttner points to the outsides that a rationalistic and instrumentalist critique would never approach, such as the historical outside to contemporary life, aesthetic judgement as a partial outside to art's institutional reality, faith as an outside to the human, and immanent categories of virtue as an outside to power.

Aber ist Büttners vorweggenommene ästhetische Verlegenheit nicht bloß eine gehemmte Form von Meta-Coolness? Eine solche Haltung unterschiede sich ironischerweise kaum von der Institutionskritik der zweiten Generation, dem Evangelium an deutschen Kunstakademien der 1990er Jahre (und Grund für Büttners Scham): wie jede Konzeptkunst, die etwas auf sich hält, braucht auch Institutionskritik einen Feind und entwickelt entsprechend eine parasitäre Beziehung zu Kunstinstitutionen – wie Büttner zum Konzept der Coolness.
Es stimmt, dass Büttners Werk eine Art Gegen-Institutionskritik ist, weil sie zum Beispiel in ihren Schriften das Konzept einer „Kunstwelt" akzeptiert, aber auch wegen ihres grundlegenden Einverständnisses mit der soziologischen Analyse über die Art und Weise, in der das Feld der Kunst und visuellen Kultur dem Kunstwerk Wert verleiht. Das belegt ihre Videoarbeit *Little Works* (2007) über englische Nonnen und deren Handarbeit, im Klosterjargon „kleine Werke" genannt, eine Arbeit, die man nur schwer als Allegorie für die narzisstischen Selbstverwirklichungsprojekte der kreativen Klasse verkennen kann. Sie verwandelt in ihrer Kunst Scham in eine performative Form, die sich um eine strategische Lesart der Kunstwelt bemüht, indem sie Subjektivität oder das „ästhetische Selbst" einsetzt. Strategisch, weil heute der Holzschnitt zum Beispiel nicht mehr als eine Sache der Achtzigerjahre betrachtet wird, die die männlichen Maler mal machten, aber jetzt unmodern ist. Holzschnitt ist nicht mehr uncool. Büttners Werk verweigert sich dem Spiel nicht völlig (auch wenn sie der Innovation als konventioneller künstlerischer Tugend ironischerweise eine bestimmte Art der Passivität vorzuziehen scheint), sondern versucht, den Einsatz zu ändern, indem sie sich weigert, dessen normative Werte zu akzeptieren. Entsprechend stellt sie ausschließen-

Artist A.: 'So you work with nuns? My God, how reactionary! I hate the Catholic Church.'
Andrea Büttner: 'Would you say the same about Islam or Buddhism?'
Artist A.: 'Oh, I'm sure that Hinduism is horrible too. All organized religion is horrible.'
Andrea Büttner: 'Oh please, unorganized religion is just psychology.'

Büttner's production differs from much contemporary art by being related neither to the tradition of the readymade, nor to any specific medium. Her project isn't constituted by the obvious references and strategies: this is her *instinct d'abandon*, her strategy for dissolving authorship. The graphic print is a block of artistic affect, and, to a certain extent, a resistance against normative determinations of contemporaneity. There is no reason to assume that a printmaking artist such as Andrea Büttner has forgotten about the relativity of artistic media and institutional theories of the art concept. Despite the relative anachronism of working with printmaking, Büttner's is a post-media practice and cannot be absorbed in a traditionalist media discourse or a metaphysics of presence: instead her works echo with images, concepts, technologies and historical events that remove the print from what it once expressed, and in this way form a knowing return to the graphic surface. What, then, is her politics of the graphic print?

The humanism of the graphic artistic media relates to mid-twentieth-century use of the print as a vehicle of the religious and existentialist worldviews of the 1950s, the counter-culture of the 1960s, and the political 1970s. One could even postulate that the graphic print constitutes a myth of origin for the aesthetics of emancipatory modernity. Unlike a musealized art and its exclusive artistic media, the graphic arts are rather associated with the intimate space of printed media – the book and the periodical – and with affordable

de Definitionen des politischen Kunstwerks ständig in Frage, wenn sie sich etwa über die Tabuisierung des Religiösen als legitimes Thema der zeitgenössischen Kunst hinwegsetzt.

Außerdem findet sich in ihren Arbeiten letztlich nichts von der moralischen Prüderie der weniger selbstreflexiven Versionen von Institutionskritik, die sich selbst für fähig hält, die Macht „an sich" bloßzustellen und anzugreifen. Wie schon erwähnt, öffnen sie sich Geschichte und Gesellschaft als ganzer, aber auch einer Analyse der Subjektivierung in der visuellen Kultur, was ihnen eine ganz andere Bandbreite verleiht. Büttner zeigt auf das Außen, dem sich eine rationalistische und instrumentalisierte Kritik nie nähern würde: das historische Außen des zeitgenössischen Lebens, das der institutionellen Realität der Kunst teilweise äußerliche ästhetische Urteil; den Glauben als das, was dem Menschen äußerlich ist, und immanente Kategorien der Tugend als das Äußerliche der Macht.

Künstler A: „Ach, du arbeitest mit Nonnen? Mein Gott, wie reaktionär. Ich hasse die katholische Kirche."
Andrea Büttner: „Würdest du dasselbe über den Islam oder den Buddhismus sagen?"
Künstler A: „Sicher ist der Hinduismus auch schrecklich. Jede organisierte Religion ist schrecklich."
Andrea Büttner: „Ich bitte dich, nicht organisierte Religion ist doch bloß Psychologie."

Büttners Produktion unterscheidet sich von Teilen der zeitgenössischen Kunst, weil sie sich weder auf die Tradition des Readymade noch auf ein spezifisches Medium bezieht. Ihr Projekt entsteht nicht aus offensichtlichen Bezügen und Strategien, und das ist ihr „instinct d'abandon", ihre Strategie zur Auflösung der Autorschaft. Die Druckgraphik ist ein Ausdruck künstlerischen Affekts und leistet

art objects for affordable art consumption, as well as with the street as the privileged site for protest and social change. Especially wood- and linocutting evoke the handout and the union poster, and other popular (and populist) forms of art and communication that kept it real. The graphic print thus evokes an epic of direct action, while already being an artistic sign.

When artists today return to such artistic media it has to do with the mobilizations and philosophies of which these media used to be the visual face, but also with the fact that handmade prints resist easy exchange in a regime of logistical and commercial abstraction. They manifest singularity and difference through glitches in the printing, and through the specific tactility that distinguishes them from photographic reproduction. In an over-visualized culture, the manually produced graphic print is a still meaningful way to make images. The graphic print cannot become a hyper-image because it is steeped in difference through the elementary procedure of the cut. But since the graphic media are elementarily reproducible and transferable in their own right, they do not symmetrically oppose the endless circulation of digitally processed images either; they are not dropouts of the media galaxy, but form sequences that, historically and structur-ally, are aligned with mass media.

Büttner's work for *Documenta 13*, *Little Sisters: Luna Park Ostia* (2012), established a notion of the spectacle that competes with more sinister and totalizing views of this concept. The installation revolves around a video about the Little Sisters of Jesus, an order of nuns that is contemplative; that is, they don't convert non-believers and they don't missionize. The Little Sisters share the lives of ordinary, secular workers by taking jobs as cleaning ladies and cashiers. Because their order was founded in the Algerian desert, they accept nomadism as a condition of life, and have historically worked with circuses and

in gewissem Maße Widerstand gegen normative Festlegungen des Zeitgemäßen. Es gibt keinen Grund anzunehmen, dass eine Künstlerin, die wie Andrea Büttner mit Druckgraphik arbeitet, die Relativität der künstlerischen Medien und institutionellen Theorien des Kunstbegriffs vergessen hätte. Trotz des relativen Anachronismus dieses Mediums folgt Büttner einer postmedialen Praxis und lässt sich nicht unter einen traditionalistischen Mediendiskurs oder eine Metaphysik der Präsenz subsumieren. Stattdessen schwingen in ihrem Werk Bilder, Konzepte, Technologien und historische Ereignisse mit, die den Druck von seinem einstigen Inhalt entfernt und ihn wissentlich zur graphischen Oberfläche zurückkehren lässt. Was also ist ihre Politik der Druckgraphik?

Der Humanismus künstlerischer druckgraphischer Medien bezieht sich auf die Zeit Mitte des 20. Jahrhunderts, als sie als Vehikel für die religiösen und existentialistischen Weltsichten der 1950er, die Gegenkultur der 1960er und die politischen 1970er Jahre dienten. Man könnte die Druckgraphik sogar als Ursprungsmythos der Ästhetik der emanzipatorischen Moderne bezeichnen. Anders als die musealisierte Kunst mit ihren exklusiven künstlerischen Medien ist die Druckkunst eher mit dem vertrauten Raum der gedruckten Medien – Buch und Zeitschrift – und mit preiswerten Kunstobjekten für preiswerten Kunstkonsum assoziiert, aber auch mit der Straße als bevorzugtem Ort des Protests und der gesellschaftlichen Veränderung. Vor allem der Holz- und Linolschnitt evozierte das Flugblatt, das Gewerkschaftsplakat und andere populäre (und populistische) Formen von Kunst und Kommunikation, die ihn am Leben hielten. Die Druckgraphik evoziert also eine Epik der direkten Aktion, ist aber gleichzeitig auch künstlerisches Zeichen.

Wenn Künstler heute auf solche Medien zurückgreifen, hat das mit den Aktionen und Philosophien zu tun, denen diese Medien ihr

Fabric Painting (blue), 2011, stretched fabric, 150 × 120 cm

funfairs. The nuns portrayed by Büttner – a group in Ostia, Italy – are the last of the Little Sisters to share the lives of funfair people. Like something out of Italo Calvino's short stories about the poor rural farmer Marcovaldo,[10] who moves to the city and tries to come to terms with modern urbanity, the Little Sisters of Jesus founded their order among yodelling Bedouins in North Africa in order to spread good vibes to the city's disenchanted louts and estranged lovers with merry-go-rounds and tombolas. In the nuns' fairground the spectacle is anything but capital-as-image that totally dominates social life (as Guy Debord's dominant definition of the term goes). Instead, the spectacle of the Little Sisters of Jesus is a non-entrepreneurial cottage industry, replete with handmade prizes and home-grown attractions.

Some nice paradoxes offer themselves up for exploration, then. The handmade print also testifies to the presence of the non-human; to the media effects, perhaps, that – to paraphrase Marshall McLuhan – work us over as humans. The non-human can also be understood in terms of depictions of threats to freedom. Think of the posters of the May 1968 Paris uprising, with their images of violent repression (riot police), abstract power (capital) and conformity (flocks of sheep). As a propaganda tool and an educator, the print has often carried images of disasters that prey on our humanity, from the bomb to unemployment, imperialism and sexism, and of course of whichever human agency might redeem them: unity, equality, emancipation, revolution and political passions, such as engagement and indignation.

In Büttner's case, the non-human is represented through signs that suggest the presence of that which culture assumes to be bigger than the individual human being. Faith would be one such topic in her oeuvre; consider for example *A stone Schwitters painted in the*

---

visuelles Gesicht verliehen, aber auch damit, dass handgemachte Drucke den problemlosen Wechsel zu einem Regime logistischer und kommerzieller Abstraktion verweigern. Sie manifestieren ihre Singularität und Differenz durch die Fehler beim Druck und durch die spezifische Haptik, die sie von photographischen Reproduktionen unterscheidet. In einer übermäßig visualisierten Kultur ist der manuell produzierte graphische Druck immer noch eine sinnvolle Art, Bilder herzustellen. Er kann nicht zum Hyper-Bild werden, weil er durch die elementare Prozedur des Schneidens von Differenz durchdrungen ist. Und doch sind die graphischen Medien an sich grundlegend reproduzierbar und übertragbar und stellen sich der endlosen Zirkulation digital verarbeitet Bilder nicht symmetrisch entgegen; sie fallen nicht aus der Mediengalaxie heraus, sondern bilden Sequenzen, die historisch und strukturell auf einer Ebene mit den Massenmedien stehen.

Büttners Arbeit für die *Documenta 13* (2012), *Little Sisters: Luna Park Ostia*, führt einen Begriff des Spektakels ein, der mit seinen eher düsteren und totalisierenden Konnotationen konkurriert. Die Installation kreist um ein Video über die Kleinen Schwestern Jesu, einen kontemplativen Nonnenorden, dessen Mitglieder Ungläubige nicht bekehren wollen und auch nicht missionieren. Die Nonnen arbeiten als Putzfrauen und Kassiererinnen und teilen so das Leben gewöhnlicher säkularer Arbeiter. Weil ihr Orden in der algerischen Wüste gegründet wurde, akzeptiert er das Nomadentum und war in seiner Geschichte im Zirkus und auf Jahrmärkten tätig. Die von Büttner – als Gruppe im italienischen Ostia – portraitierten Nonnen leben mit den Leuten vom Jahrmarkt. Als seien sie der Kurzgeschichte von Italo Calvino über den armen Bauern Marcovaldo entsprungen, der in die Stadt zieht und versucht, mit der modernen Urbanität zurechtzukommen, gründeten die Kleinen Schwestern

Fabric Painting (neon orange), 2011, stretched fabric, 150 × 120 cm

Lake District (2005), a large woodcut of a potato-like, oval shape divided into wide, colourful zebra stripes and hovering mysteriously against a black background. *A stone...* is like an incantation of all the questions that art can raise – here predicated on Dada frontman Kurt Schwitters: why did he paint a stone in the Lake District? What was he doing there in the first place? Did the stone really look like this? Did such a stone ever exist? The answers are as elusive, as Schwitters' stone palpably lies in your hand.

Strung out between the human and the non-human, mechanical reproduction and direct agency, art making and mass media, the print is the art form that cannot hide its means of production, its specific materiality. Jacques Lacan's concept of extimacy is pertinent here, perhaps.[11] According to Lacan, the extimate is an estrangement that exists in extreme proximity to oneself. It is that which is intimate to one's self, yet alien to who one is: feelings of shame, powerlessness or impotence, say. The print can be seen as extimate to the capitalist spectacle, as a strange untimely image that shares some of the spectacle's fundamental traits.

A copy is not a copy is not a copy is...

Don't look at me any more

In Büttner, subjective discomfort is inextricably bound up with specific historical conditions; that is, with existing social space and visual culture. Discomfort doesn't stem from inherent physical traits or the artist being a genius, or a misfit, or a madwoman, or any other kind of radical and trans-historical subject, but rather from interaction with certain discourses and cultural givens.

There is little symbolic surplus value in referring to Milan Kundera's Indo-European brand of post-existentialist meta-fiction. The old

---

Jesu ihren Orden unter singenden Beduinen in Nordafrika, um bei desillusionierten Rüpeln und getrennten Liebenden durch Karussell und Tombola gute Stimmung zu verbreiten. Auf dem Jahrmarkt der Nonnen ist das Spektakel alles andere als das Kapital-als-Bild, das das gesellschaftliche Leben völlig dominiert (wie Guy Debord den Begriff definierte). Das Spektakel der Kleinen Schwestern Jesu ist statt dessen nichtunternehmerische Heimarbeit, voller handgefertigter Gewinne und selbstgemachter Attraktionen.

Es bieten sich also ein paar hübsche Paradoxa für die Untersuchung an. Der handgemachte Druck bezeugt auch die Präsenz des Nichtmenschlichen, die Medieneffekte vielleicht, die – um McLuhan zu zitieren – uns als Menschen massieren. Man denke an die Plakate der Pariser Mai-Demonstrationen von 1968 mit ihren Bilder von gewalttätiger Unterdrückung (Bereitschaftspolizei), abstrakter Macht (Kapital) und Konformität (Schafherden). Als Werkzeug der Propaganda und Erziehung haben Drucke oft Bilder von Katastrophen gezeigt, die unsere Menschlichkeit bedrohen, von der Bombe bis zu Arbeitslosigkeit, Imperialismus und Sexismus, aber natürlich auch von der jeweiligen menschlichen Kraft, die uns davon erlösen soll: Einheit, Gleichheit, Emanzipation, Revolution und politische Leidenschaften wie Engagement und Empörung.

In Büttners Fall wird das Nichtmenschliche durch Zeichen repräsentiert, die auf das verweisen, was die Kultur für größer hält als den individuellen Menschen. Der Glaube wäre ein solches Thema in ihrem Œuvre; als Beispiel kann man *A stone Schwitters painted in the Lake District* (2008) betrachten, ein großer Holzschnitt, der eine kartoffelartige, ovale Form zeigt, die in breite, farbige Zebrastreifen unterteilt ist und geheimnisvoll vor schwarzem Hintergrund schwebt. *A Stone...* ist wie eine Beschwörung all der

ponce won't get an obituary in *Frieze* when his time is up. So let us retrace homeopathically and go *back* to Kundera, who has more to say on the matter of shame. He writes in *Immortality* (1991): 'The basis of shame is not some personal mistake of ours, but the ignominy, the humiliation we feel that we must be what we are without any choice in the matter, and that this humiliation is seen by everyone.'[12]

To Kundera, this humiliation is connected with discovering one's physical self for the first time: the first and most important feeling that comes over one is shame. Yes, according to Kundera even a beautiful person is 'as ashamed as a toy with a long green nose' about their physical appearance, because beauty reveals the non-individuality of a face, hence the handsome person finds it difficult to believe that what they are seeing in the mirror 'is an inimitable self'.[13]

Considering the empirical evidence of the many smug, good-looking people in the world, this point is rather too philosophical. True, physiognomy is destiny, as Nietzsche said, but that is something entirely different. If we – by mixing Kundera with Nietzsche – can agree that physiognomy is often shameful, we get to the fact that shame is a poignant, yet unwilled and rather painful subjectivation: a certain intuition of what is our individual – literally *indivisible* – destiny.

Shame is a disproportionate affect. Whereas other kinds of affect are usually bigger than the subject, shame is felt squarely within the bounds of the self – yes, it re-traces these boundaries and makes them impossible to transgress. It is an overpowering feeling that is small to everybody else. It diminishes a person by making them stand out: 'So this is what I am, nothing more. This is how I am unfit for the image I have created for myself. Don't look

Fragen, die die Kunst aufwerfen kann – hier gegründet auf den DADA-Künstler Kurt Schwitters: Warum hat er im Lake District einen Stein bemalt? Was hat er da überhaupt gemacht? Hat der Stein wirklich so ausgesehen? Hat es einen solchen Stein je gegeben? Die Antworten sind so schwer zu fassen wie Schwitters Stein spürbar in der Hand liegt.

Der Druck, der zwischen dem Menschlichen und dem Nichtmenschlichen schwebt, zwischen maschineller Reproduktion und direkter Aktion, Kunstproduktion und Massenmedien, ist die Kunstform, die ihre Beziehungen zur Produktion, ihre spezifische Materialität nicht verbergen kann. Vielleicht passt hier Jacques Lacans Konzept der Extimität. Laut Lacan ist das Extime eine Entfremdung, die in extremer Nähe zum Selbst steht. Es ist das, was dem Selbst intim ist, und doch dem fremd, wer man ist: das Gefühl von Scham, Machtlosigkeit oder Impotenz. So kann auch der Druck als dem kapitalistischen Spektakel extim betrachtet werden, als seltsam unzeitgemäßes Bild mit einigen grundlegenden Merkmalen des Spektakels.

Eine Kopie ist keine Kopie ist keine Kopie ist ...

Sieh mich nicht mehr an

Bei Büttner ist subjektives Unbehagen unlösbar mit spezifischen historischen Bedingungen verbunden, das heißt, mit dem existierenden gesellschaftlichen Raum und der visuellen Kultur. Unbehagen entsteht nicht aus inhärenten körperlichen Merkmalen oder der Tatsache, dass die Künstlerin ein Genie, ein Freak, eine Verrückte oder irgendein anderes radikales und geschichtsübergreifendes Objekt ist, sondern aus der Interaktion mit bestimmten Diskursen und kulturellen Gegebenheiten.

at me any more.' If an orgasm is a small death, shame originates and explodes on the same terrain of the self, as an involuntary self-abandonment. If it isn't too Kundera-like to put it like this, you could say that shame is an orgasm in reverse.

It can be argued that Kundera's theodicy of shit not only belittles religion, but that it is also symptomatic of our culture's growing incapacity to deal with death. Death is abstraction per se, if we by abstraction understand that which is unavailable to the senses. In Büttner's prints, the abstract expanses between text and image is death that rubs against life, value, and the ways in which we believe in things.

To embrace our shame and to cultivate our instinct for letting go is how we may give death its faces back, and how we may give existing society an outside.

1

Milan Kundera, *The Unbearable Lightness of Being*, originally published in French as *L'insoutenable légèreté de l'être*, Gallimard, Paris, 1984. Trans. Michael Henry Heim, Harper Collins, New York, 1984, p. 246.

2

Theodor Adorno, *Minima Moralia. Reflections from Damaged Life*, Verso, London, 2005 (1971), p. 49.

3

Scott Andrews, 'Andrea Büttner at Artpace', *San Antonio Current*, 10 August 2011. Available online at http://sacurrent.com/arts/visualart/andrea-büttner-at-artpace-1.1186228.

4

Cf. Dexter Bang Sinister, 'Good Shit', in Dexter Bang Sinister, eds., *Bulletins of the Serving Library #4*, Dexter Sinister, 2012.

5

Siouxsie and the Banshees, *The Last Beat of My Heart*, 1988.

6

Andrea Büttner, *Perspectives on Shame and Art: Warhol, Sedgwick, Freud and Roth,* unpublished PhD dissertation, Royal College of Art, London, 2008, p. 13 and p. 25.

7

Ibid., iii.

Es hat wenig symbolischen Mehrwert, auf Milan Kunderas indo-europäische Version postexistenzialistischer Metafiktion hinzuweisen. Der alte Schöngeist wird keinen Nachruf in *Frieze* bekommen, wenn seine Zeit um ist. Kehren wir also in homöopathischen Schritten um und kommen auf Kundera „zurück", der mehr über die Scham zu sagen hat. Er schreibt in *Unsterblichkeit* (1990): „Die Grundlage der Scham ist nicht irgendein persönlicher Fehler, sondern die Schande, die Erniedrigung, die wir dafür empfinden, daß wir sein müssen, was wir sind, ohne daß wir es uns so ausgesucht haben, und es ist das unerträgliche Gefühl, daß diese Erniedrigung von überall zu sehen ist."[10]

Für Kundera ist diese Erniedrigung mit der ersten Entdeckung des eigenen körperlichen Ichs verbunden: das erste und wichtigste Gefühl, das einen dabei überkommt, ist die Scham. Für Kundera schämt sich sogar ein schöner Mensch seiner körperlichen Erscheinung genauso, wie sich ein Spielzeugmännchen mit langer grüner Nase für sein Gesicht schämt, denn die Schönheit offenbart „das Un-Persönliche" eines Gesichts, und deswegen kann ein schöner Mensch „schwerlich glauben, daß das, was er [im Spiegel] sieht, irgendein originelles Ich sein soll."[11]

Berücksichtigt man die nachweislich große Zahl gutaussehender eingebildeter Menschen auf der Welt, dürfte das eine allzu philosophische Behauptung sein. Sicher ist Physiognomie Schicksal, wie Nietzsche sagt, aber das ist etwas ganz anderes. Wenn wir uns – durch eine Mischung aus Kundera und Nietzsche – darauf einigen können, dass Physiognomie oft beschämt, kommen wir zu der Tatsache, dass Scham eine eindringliche, aber ungewollte und eher schmerzliche Subjektivierung ist: eine gewisse intuitive Einsicht in unser individuelles – buchstäblich „unteilbares" – Schicksal.

8
Andrea Büttner in Gil Leung, 'Artists at
Work: Andrea Büttner', *Afterall Online*, 2010.
Available at: http://www.afterall.org/online/
artists.at.workandreabttner.
9
Milan Kundera, *Immortality*. Faber and
Faber, London, 1991, p. 330.
10
Italo Calvino, *Marcovaldo ovvero Le stagioni
in città (Marcovaldo, or The Seasons in the
City)*, Harcourt Brace & Company, Orlando
1983 (1963).
11
Jacques Lacan. *The Seminar. Book VII. The
Ethics of Psychoanalysis*, 1959–60. Trans.
Dennis Porter. Routledge, London 1992,
p. 139.
12
Milan Kundera, *Immortality*. Faber and
Faber, London, 1991, p. 276.
13
Ibid., p. 277.

Scham ist ein unverhältnismäßiger Affekt. Während andere Affek-
te in der Regel größer sind als das Subjekt, wird Scham innerhalb
der Grenzen des Selbst empfunden – sie umreißt diese Grenzen
sogar noch und macht ein Überschreiten unmöglich. Sie lässt einen
schrumpfen, indem sie einen hervorhebt: „Das also ist es, was ich
bin, und nicht mehr. So bin ich,
und ich passe nicht zu dem Bild, das ich selbst geschaffen habe.
Seht mich nicht mehr an." Wenn ein Orgasmus ein kleiner Tod ist,
dann beginnt und explodiert die Scham als unfreiwillige Selbst-
aufgabe im selben Bereich des Selbst. Wenn es nicht zu sehr nach
Kundera klänge, könnte man sagen, Scham ist ein umgekehrter
Orgasmus.
Man könnte behaupten, dass Kunderas Theodizee der Scheiße
nicht nur die Religion verspottet, sondern auch ein Symptom
für die wachsende Unfähigkeit unserer Kultur ist, mit dem
Tod umzugehen. Der Tod ist die Abstraktion an sich, wenn wir
unter Abstraktion das verstehen, was den Sinnen nicht zugäng-
lich ist. In Büttners Druckgraphiken sind die abstrakten Bereiche
zwischen Text und Bild der Tod, der sich am Leben reibt, am
Wert und an der Art unseres Glaubens.
Vielleicht müssen wir die Scham annehmen und den Instinkt
zum Loslassen kultivieren, um dem Tod sein Gesicht zurück- und
der existierenden Gesellschaft ein Außen zu geben.

1
Milan Kundera (1984), *Die unerträgliche
Leichtigkeit des Seins*. Aus dem
Tschechischen von Susanna Roth.
München 2004, S. 225.

2
Theodor W. Adorno (1951), *Minima
Moralia*. Frankfurt am Main 2001, S. 78.

Benches, 2012, handwoven fabric, wood, plastic crates, 45.8 × 200 × 40 cm,
each bench; 200 × 42 × 5 cm, each back.
Installation view, International Project Space.

3
http://sacurrent.com/arts/visualart/andrea-
büttner-at-artpace-1.1186228
4
Vgl. Dexter Bang Sinister, "Good Shit", in
ders. (Hg.): *Bulletins of the Serving Library 4*,
New York City 2012.
5
Siouxsie and the Banshees: *The Last Beat
of My Heart* (1988).
6
Andrea Büttner, *Perspectives on Shame and
Art: Warhol, Sedgwick, Freud and Roth.*
Unveröffentlichte Dissertation (Royal
College of Art, London 2008), S. 13 und 25.
7
A.a.O., S. iii.
8
Andrea Büttner in Gil Leung, "Artists at
Work: Andrea Büttner", *Afterall Online*,
2010. Zitiert nach der Online-Version:
http://www.afterall.org/online/artists.
at.workandreabüttner (7. Juni 2012).
9
Milan Kundera, *Die Unsterblichkeit*. Aus
dem Tschechischen von Susanna Roth,
München/Wien 1990, S. 358.
10
Kundera 1990, S. 301.
11
Ebd.

Benches, 2011, wood, plastic crates, 45.8 × 200 × 80 cm
Corner Seat, 2011, wood, plastic crates, 45.8 × 400 × 80 cm

Grille, 2007, woodcut, 113 × 180 cm

Dancing Nuns, 2007, woodcut, 113 × 180 cm

Nativity, 2007, woodcut, triptych, 179.5 × 90 cm, each sheet

Dancing Nuns, 2007, woodcut, diptych, 180 × 113 cm, each sheet

Dancing Nuns (miracle), 2007, mono print, 60.5 × 76 cm

A stone Schwitters painted in the Lake District, 2005, woodcut, 95 × 140 cm

A stone Schwitters painted in the Lake District

ARTWORK AS DIVESTMENT
POVERTY, AND THE WORK OF ANDREA BÜTTNER
Richard Birkett

The collection of the Museum für Moderne Kunst, Frankfurt, includes a work by the US artist Laurie Parsons titled *Pieces* and dated 1989.[1] In the MMK's online archive, *Pieces* is pictured installed under what appears to be a stairwell.[2] Defined spatially by a wedge-shaped corner, and the shadow cast by the ascending stairs overhead, the work comprises an arrangement of urban detritus – an empty paint can, half a brick, and a metal pipe, alongside unrecognizable, seemingly crushed items of waste. The objects appear 'scattered', with far less formal specificity than the fields of material symptomatic of the late 1960s post-minimalist works also featured in the museum's collection.

Laurie Parsons was active as an exhibiting artist between 1986 and 1993. A chronicle of her 'career' written by the curator and writer Bob Nickas, titled 'Demateral Girl', outlines her production and exhibition history year by year, and her steps towards a self-professed realization that 'art must spread into other realms, into spirituality and social giving'.[3] In 1994 Parsons made a conscious break from the art world, choosing instead to apply herself to forms of social work.

'Demateral Girl' provides an overview of a practice that eschewed production as such, and instead took its initial cue from pre-existing, impoverished objecthood. Parsons' early gallery exhibitions comprised groupings of waste found during walks across natural, industrial and urban areas. This procedure did not solely revolve around the assigning of aesthetic value to discarded matter; the development of her work suggested otherwise, that

DAS KUNSTWERK ALS ENTKLEIDUNG:
ARMUT IM WERK VON ANDREA BÜTTNER
Richard Birkett

In der Sammlung des MMK Museum für Moderne Kunst in Frankfurt gibt es ein Werk der amerikanischen Künstlerin Laurie Parsons mit dem Titel *Pieces* von 1989.[1] Wie das Bild im Online-Archiv des MMK zeigt, wurde *Pieces* unter einem Treppenabsatz installiert.[2] Räumlich durch eine keilförmige Ecke und den Schatten der Treppenstufen definiert, sieht man ein Arrangement aus städtischem Abfall – eine leere Farbdose, einen halben Ziegelstein und ein Metallrohr neben unkenntlichen, vielleicht zerdrückten Abfallstücken. Die Objekte wirken „verstreut", formal weit weniger spezifisch als die post-minimalistischen Werke der späten 1960er Jahre in derselben Sammlung.

Laurie Parsons hat in den Jahren 1986 bis 1993 ausgestellt. Eine Chronik ihrer „Karriere", die der Kurator und Autor Bob Nickas unter dem Titel „Demateral Girl" zusammengestellt hat[3], dokumentiert Jahr für Jahr die Geschichte ihrer Werke und Ausstellungen und die einzelnen Schritte zu ihrer Erkenntnis, Kunst müsse „in andere Bereiche vordringen, in Spiritualität und soziale Hingabe". 1994 brach Parsons bewusst mit der Kunstwelt und arbeitet seitdem im sozialen Bereich.

„Demateral Girl" bietet einen Überblick über eine Arbeitsweise, die auf Produktion als solche verzichtete und sich stattdessen an bereits vorhandenen, gebrauchten und weggeworfenen Objekten orientierte. In ihren frühen Galerieausstellungen zeigte Parsons Arrangements aus Abfall, den sie bei Wanderungen in der Natur, in Industriegebieten und Städten gesammelt hatte. Dabei ging es nicht allein darum, weggeworfenen Materialien ästhetischen Wert

HAP Grieshaber / Franz Fühmann: Engel der Geschichte 25: Engel der Behinderten, Classen Verlag Düsseldorf 1982, (HAP Grieshaber / Franz Fühmann: Angel of History 25: Angel of the Disabled), 2010, Xerox and clip frames, 42 × 59.2 cm, each

in fact it was the material and social relations formed through her actions within the gallery that were of primary interest. A solo exhibition in 1990 presented an empty gallery, with a blank invitation card save for the gallery name, address and telephone number.[4] Parsons states: 'I felt it essential that I consider the gallery itself, rather than continue to unquestioningly use it as a context. With its physical space and intricate social organization, it is as real, and as meaningful, as the artwork it houses and markets.'[5]

If this effacing of the presence of productivity forms a self-reflexive questioning of the value of (art)work as a social 'good' within the narrative of Parsons' career, two works executed at the New Museum in the early 1990s exist as tipping points. In one instance she placed a four-inch stack of dollar bills in the gallery, telling the museum guards not to interfere if visitors chose to remove the money.[6] And as part of the group show *The Spatial Drive*, Parsons proposed that the exhibition do without conventional modes of mediation, such as a brochure or wall labels, and instead place the emphasis on communication between the gallery attendants and visitors.[7] The necessary inclusion of the security and admissions staff in the exhibition planning process, and in discussions with artists, was maintained by the museum for several years after the exhibition.[8]

The seven-year arc of Parsons' artistic production can be read as one of divestment – she engaged in progressive acts of relinquishing the conventional 'assets' an artist holds: the creation of artworks that attain market value, the maintenance of the gallery space as a site of privileged access, and the authorial voice as primary mediator of the work and its reception. This divestiture was coupled with the implied transference of such assets

zuzuschreiben. Vielmehr zeigt die Entwicklung ihres Werks, dass sie sich vor allem für die materiellen und sozialen Beziehungen interessierte, die durch ihre Aktionen in den Ausstellungsräumen entstanden. 1990 präsentierte sie in einer Einzelausstellung leere Räume; auf den Einladungskarten standen nur Name, Adresse und Telefonnummer der Galerie.[4] Sie selbst sagte dazu: „Mir schien es wesentlich, die Galerie selbst zu berücksichtigen, statt sie unhinterfragt weiterhin als Kontext zu benutzen. Mit ihrem physischen Raum und ihrer komplexen sozialen Struktur ist sie genauso wirklich und bedeutend wie die Kunstwerke, die sie beherbergt und vermarktet."[5]

Wenn diese Tilgung von Produktivität den Wert des (Kunst-) Werks als soziale „Ware" im Narrativ ihrer künstlerischen Laufbahn in Frage stellt, so markieren zwei Werke, die Parsons Anfang der 1990er Jahre im New Museum zeigte, den Wendepunkt. Zum einen legte sie einen 10 Zentimeter hohen Stapel von Dollarscheinen in den Ausstellungsraum, mit der Anweisung an das Aufsichtspersonal, nicht einzugreifen, wenn Besucher sich das Geld nahmen.[6] Zum anderen machte sie im Rahmen der Gruppenausstellung *The Spatial Drive* den Vorschlag, auf konventionelle Vermittlungsformen wie Broschüren oder Wandbeschriftungen zu verzichten und stattdessen die Kommunikation zwischen Aufsichtspersonal und Besuchern zu fördern.[7] Das Museum hat die dadurch notwendig gewordene Beteiligung des Aufsichts- und Kassenpersonals an der Planung der Ausstellungen und der Diskussion mit den Künstlern noch jahrelang nach der Ausstellung weitergeführt.[8]

Parsons sieben Jahre dauernde künstlerische Produktion lässt sich als eine Kurve der Entäußerung verstehen – als schrittweises Aufgeben der üblichen „Aktivposten" eines Künstlers: die Kunstwerke,

HAP Grieshaber / Franz Fühmann: Engel der Geschichte 25: Engel der Behinderten, Classen Verlag Düsseldorf 1982, (HAP Grieshaber / Franz Fühmann: Angel of History 25: Angel of the Disabled), 2010

to others, a tendency that ultimately found its resolution in Parsons' complete turn to 'social giving'.

Laying out such a narrative around Laurie Parsons' trajectory as an artist is not intended as a platform from which to make direct connections between her work and that of Andrea Büttner, the principal subject of this text. *Pieces,* as a recalcitrant tangible artefact of an artistic practice that ultimately cast off physical matter to address material and social supports through immateriality, however, serves as a lightning rod for a constellation of concerns around critical judgement, art's social potential, and notions of wilful poverty, activated through the hagiographic chronicling of Parsons' disavowal of the 'art world'. It is at this allegorical juncture of apophatic values, exemplified by the material and social-symbolic constitution of the work of art and its reception, that Andrea Büttner's practice functions. Her exhibitions extend from the specificity and volatility of the art gallery as a space of codified judgement, and dialectically the affective and political potential in the act of showing, and the reciprocity this provokes. Poverty, as a material, social and emotional state of being that reaches beyond critical detachment, exists at the heart of the relations within her work.

Büttner's 2011 exhibitions at the Whitechapel Gallery in London, and the Collezione Maramotti in Reggio Emilia, Italy, both assumed the title *The Poverty of Riches*, taken from a publication by theologian Kenneth Baxter Wolf on St. Francis of Assisi.[9] The exhibitions comprised a number of two-dimensional works – woodcut prints, paintings on glass, photographs, and raw fabric canvases – alongside a small pile of apples in a corner of the gallery, and a series of benches, simply constructed from two grey plastic

die einen Marktwert erzielen, den Ausstellungsraum als Ort privilegierten Zugangs und die Stimme des Urhebers als primärem Vermittler des Werks und seiner Rezeption, gepaart mit der impliziten Übertragung dieser Aktivposten auf andere. Am Ende stand der vollständige Wechsel zur „sozialen Hingabe".

Diese Skizze über Laurie Parsons Weg als Künstlerin soll keineswegs einem direkten Vergleich ihres Werks mit dem von Andrea Büttner, um das es in diesem Text vor allem geht, das Wort reden. Aber als widerständiges, greifbares Artefakt einer künstlerischen Praxis, die letztlich das physische Material zugunsten einer Beschäftigung mit Materialität und Sozialität durch Immaterialität aufgibt, zeigt *Pieces* exemplarisch, welche Fragen zum kritischen Urteil, zum sozialen Potential der Kunst und zu Vorstellungen freiwilliger Armut die hagiographische Chronik der Trennung der Künstlerin von der „Kunstwelt" aufwirft. An diesem allegorischen Schnittpunkt aus negativen Werten, verdeutlicht durch die materielle und sozial-symbolische Struktur des Kunstwerks und seiner Rezeption, setzt die Arbeit von Andrea Büttner an. Ihre Ausstellungen umfassen den so spezifischen wie flüchtigen Raum der Kunstgalerie als Ort des kodifizierten Urteils genauso wie die Dialektik des affektiven und politischen Potentials im Akt des Ausstellens und die dadurch ausgelöste Reziprozität. Das Herzstück der Beziehungen innerhalb ihres Werks ist Armut als materieller, sozialer und emotionaler Seinszustand, der über die kritische Distanz hinausgeht.

Die Ausstellungen, die Büttner 2011 in der Whitechapel Gallery, London, und der Collezione Maramotti in Reggio Emilia, Italien, zeigte, waren beide nach dem Buch des Theologen Kenneth Baxter Wolf über den Heiligen Franz von Assisi[9] mit *The Poverty of Riches*

HAP Grieshaber / Franz Fühmann: Engel der Geschichte 25: Engel der Behinderten, Classen Verlag Düsseldorf 1982, (HAP Grieshaber / Franz Fühmann: Angel of History 25: Angel of the Disabled), 2010

crates and a length of timber. The collation of works was distinctly relational; a dialogue forming between seemingly incidental actions and openly crafted art objects. Across Büttner's practice an equivalent holistic attitude exists, in which recurring motifs and methodologies possess distinct functions within her process of exhibition making. As a viewer one is often conscious of the division between gestures of self-contextualization that Büttner enacts within a space – alluding to its architecture and its social fabric, and the artist's own presence within these structures – and that which is displayed as an 'external' mode of production. The gallery bench, as both an existing extension of the gallery architecture and a contrived prop, has come to play a significant role within this lexicon. Initially appearing in Büttner's exhibitions in the form of institutional furniture, the benches were co-opted within an artistic schema through their use as informal stands for a tape deck and headphones, a support system for focused listening to sound works such as *Roth Reading* (2006). In the context of *The Poverty of Riches*, the crude make-do-and-mend benches served a conventional purpose as seating for gallery visitors, yet also presented themselves as sculptural objects: in one instance they were stacked against the gallery wall, emphasizing their mini-malist seriality, and in another they were reconstituted to form a corner bench, their modularity further highlighting the repetition of a formal motif.

The benches' transitions between states of functionality and aes-thetic objecthood hinged around the act of contemplation; the gallery bench after all is not merely furniture for resting, a bodily prop, but a prompt towards an extended aesthetic and critical consideration. When stacked against the wall, the wood and plastic crate assemblage moved from the realm of the subject to become

betitelt. Sie bestanden aus einer Reihe zweidimensionaler Werke – Holzschnitte, Glasmalerei, Fotos und Leinwände aus unbehandel-tem Stoff. Zudem gab es einen kleinen Haufen Äpfel in einer Ecke der Galerie und eine Reihe einfacher Bänke, die aus zwei Plastik-kisten und einem Brett bestanden. In der Zusammenstellung waren die Werke eindeutig aufeinander bezogen; scheinbar zufällige Aktionen und erkennbar gefertigte Kunstobjekte traten in einen Dialog. Eine vergleichbar holistische Haltung, die wiederkehrenden Motiven und Methoden distinkte Funktionen im Ausstellungs-prozess zuweist, zieht sich durch Büttners gesamte Arbeit. Für den Betrachter wird die Trennung zwischen ihren Gesten der Selbst-Kontextualisierung im Raum – die auf seine Architektur und sein soziales Gefüge sowie auf die Anwesenheit der Künstlerin darin hinweisen – und dem Ausgestellten als „externem" Modus der Pro-duktion oft erkennbar.

Die Ausstellungsbank, ob als Erweiterung der Ausstellungsarchitek-tur oder als gefertigtes Requisit, spielt in diesem Vokabular eine wichtige Rolle. Büttner hat die Bänke, die in ihren Ausstellungen ursprünglich als Objektmöbel auftauchten, künstlerisch kooptiert, indem sie sie als informelle Ständer für Tonbandgerät und Kopf-hörer nutzte, als Hilfsmittel für das fokussierte Zuhören bei Klang-arbeiten wie *Roth Reading* (2006). Im Kontext von *The Poverty of Riches* erfüllten die einfachen, provisorischen Bänke ihren „konven-tionellen" Zweck als Sitzgelegenheit für Besucher, präsentierten sich aber auch als skulpturale Objekte: zum einen wurden sie an der Wand aufgestapelt, was ihre minimalistische Serialität betonte, und zum anderen zu einer Eckbank zusammengesetzt, deren Modula-rität ein formales Motiv zusätzlich wiederholte.

Der Bedeutungswechsel der Bank vom Funktionsmöbel zum ästhe-tischem Objekt und umgekehrt kreiste um den Akt der Kontem-

HAP Grieshaber / Franz Fühmann: Engel der Geschichte 25: Engel der Behinderten, Classen Verlag Düsseldorf 1982, (HAP Grieshaber / Franz Fühmann: Angel of History 25: Angel of the Disabled), 2010

the object of contemplation. Such transitions are a recurring aspect of Büttner's exhibitions, constituted around 'showing' and 'viewing' not simply as inherent functions of the gallery space, but as a series of formal, bodily and affective relations entwined with the rhetoric of display. While the benches registered transitions in their status through permutations in their placement and configuration, as a visitor to Büttner's exhibitions one is often conscious of a scenography that emphasizes a physical and phenomenological sense of location in relation to the work. In the case of *The Poverty of Riches*, the benches occupied a role as a priori mediators of aesthetic experience, in place in order to 'enable' a state of contemplation – in their crude, yet formally precise production, however, they suggested the theatrical lacing of this privileged mode of reception with asceticism and humility.

Büttner's consideration of the qualifications and mediations of the gallery space does not singularly constitute a critique of the institution of art as an interpellating force. Rather, within her work there is an emphasis on the architectural and ideological ground of the exhibition as embedded in the act of making something public; a mechanism of exposure and judgement that can be seen as a reciprocal experience between artist and viewer. Her actions in relation to this ground consistently embrace awkwardness or abjection, present either through direct depiction[10] or through gestures that implicate a perceptual or psychological 'falling down'.[11]

This is perhaps most evident in Büttner's use of the corner, as a spatial feature of the 'white cube' that she often emphasizes in her exhibitions, and as a motif that appears in a number of her two-dimensional works. In *The Poverty of Riches*, the siting of a bench (*Corner Seat*, 2011) and a small pile of apples (*Apples*, 2011) in two

plation, ist doch die Bank in einer Ausstellung nicht nur Möbel zum Ausruhen, Stütze des Körpers, sondern auch eine Aufforderung zur umfassenden ästhetischen und kritischen Betrachtung. An der Wand aufgestapelt, verließ die Assemblage aus Holz und Plastik-kiste den Bereich des Subjekts und wurde zum Objekt der Kontemplation. Solche Wechsel gibt es in Büttners Ausstellungen immer wieder; sie sind nicht nur funktional gemeint, sondern öffnen die Unterscheidung zwischen „Zeigen" und „Sehen" für eine Reihe von formalen, physischen und affektiven Beziehungen, die mit der Rhetorik des Ausstellungs-Displays verflochten sind.

So wie die Bänke durch den Wechsel der Platzierung und Konfiguration den Übergang vom Ausstellungsmöbel zum Kunstwerk anzeigen, so wird man sich auch als Besucher in Büttners Ausstellungen oft einer Rauminszenierung bewusst, die ein physisches und phänomenologisches Gefühl für das Verhältnis von Raum und Werk vermittelt. In *The Poverty of Riches* spielten die Bänke eine Rolle als a priori-Vermittler ästhetischer Erfahrung, die durch ihre Existenz einen Zustand der Kontemplation „ermöglichten", aber durch ihre primitive, wenn auch formal präzise Konstruktion auch auf die theatralische Verknüpfung dieser privilegierten Form der Rezeption mit Askese und Demut verwiesen.

Büttners Berücksichtigung der Eigenheiten und Vermittlungsweisen des Ausstellungsraumes ist mehr als nur eine Kritik an der institutionellen Kunst als interpellierende Kraft. Sie betont in ihrer Arbeit vielmehr die architektonischen und ideologischen Grundlagen der Ausstellung, die im Akt des Öffentlich-Machens liegen; im Mechanismus von Enthüllung und Urteil, der sich als reziproke Erfahrung von Künstlerin und Betrachter verstehen lässt. Ihre auf diese Grundlagen bezogenen Aktionen bejahen stets Unbeholfenheit und Abjektion. Dies wird entweder durch direkte Darstellung[10] oder

different corners of the exhibition space, alongside a woodcut of three brightly-coloured planes meeting to create a corner (*Corner*, 2011), constituted a series of shifting relations between architecture, artwork and viewer. The corner bench invited the viewer to sit and look back into the space, subverting a conventional perspective on the exhibition. This positioning of the viewer 'in the corner' also echoed rituals of social banishment, engendering psychological resonances of shame that meshed with the impoverished construction of the furniture – the self-awareness of being perceived as 'lower' both socially and materially. *Apples* registered similar connotations of shamefulness, articulated in this instance not through the positioning of the viewer, but by the symbolism of the fruit and its placement – the apple as the mythical site of original sin, combining with the fallen aspect of the corner pile to connote lowness and humbling. And while the woodcut *Corner* required a reversion to a conventional mode of 'upright' pictorial perception, its colourful, formal simplicity activated an iconographic reflexivity towards the corner as having both 'real' and symbolic functions within the exhibition.

Across these three instances the figure of the corner assumed shifting agency in its presence as material: from the corner as subject matter in the woodcut, to the corner as a constituent material within *Apples*, and as a structural support in *Corner Seat*. The onus on the corner as an operative form, both material and symbolic, framed a series of actions occurring in the realms of artistic production and reception. These actions seemed implicitly structured around counterposed levels of labour and passivity, valuing and devaluing: as a craft emblematic of anachronistic physical process, and as such perceived as critically undermined, the woodcut carried devotional qualities in its laborious creation of an iconographic

durch Gesten sichtbar, die auf ein perzeptuelles oder psychologisches „Fallen" verweisen.[11]

Am deutlichsten wird das vielleicht in Büttners Nutzung der Ecke als räumlichem Merkmal des „White Cube", das sie in ihren Ausstellungen oft betont, das aber auch als Motiv in einer Reihe ihrer zweidimensionalen Werke auftaucht. In *The Poverty of Riches* entstand durch die Platzierung einer Bank (*Corner Seat*, 2011) und eines kleinen Haufen Äpfels (*Apples*, 2011) in zwei verschiedenen Ecken des Ausstellungsraums, in Verbindung mit einem Holzschnitt, der drei leuchtend farbige Flächen zeigt, die an ihren Schnittpunkten eine Ecke bilden (*Corner*, 2011), eine Reihe wechselnder Beziehungen zwischen Architektur, Kunstwerk und Betrachter. Die Eckbank lud den Betrachter ein, sich zu setzen, in den Raum zurückzublicken und damit den konventionellen Blick auf die Ausstellung zu unterlaufen. Diese Positionierung des Betrachters „in der Ecke" wiederholte auch Rituale des sozialen Ausschlusses, in denen ein psychisches Echo der Scham mitschwang, das sich mit der ärmlichen Konstruktion des Möbels mischte – das Gefühl, im sozialen wie materiellen Sinne als „niedriger" wahrgenommen zu werden. *Apples* wies ähnliche Konnotationen von Beschämung auf, die sich hier nicht durch die Positionierung des Betrachters, sondern durch den Symbolismus der Frucht und ihres Standorts artikulierten – als mythischer Ort der Erbsünde, verbunden mit dem Aspekt des Fallens (die aufgehäuften Äpfel in der Ecke), ist der Apfel mit Geringschätzung und Demütigung konnotiert. Und während der Holzschnitt *Corner* die Rückkehr zur konventionellen, „aufrechten" bildlichen Wahrnehmung erforderte, aktivierte seine farbige, formale Schlichtheit eine ikonographische Reflexion über die gleichzeitig „reale" und symbolische Funktion der Ecke in der Ausstellung.

abstraction. The corner bench served as a relatively passive artistic gesture that framed contemplation as an uncomfortable parallel to critical judgement. And *Apples* located the viewer's decision to enter into a transaction – to take an apple or not – at the centre of its productive potential. The symbolic ground of the corner, its associations with awkwardness and shame, emanated into these actions as social forms of judgement – the mutable valuation of work and its basis in an entwined relationship with an established critical order.

The archival image of Laurie Parsons' *Pieces* shows the work wedged into a corner defined by a stairwell. The awkwardness of the location suggests a conscious decision to place the piece in a liminal site beyond the conventional arena of the gallery. The objects that constitute *Pieces* have clearly fallen out of systems of use and exchange, their conspicuous devaluation heightening the severity of a contextual shift between the 'real' world, and the context of the art gallery, and emphasizing the contingency of the definition of 'material' in relation to these structures.

Parsons' process of gathering and presenting 'things' involved a transitory phase during which the objects would be kept at the artist's studio, and 'lived with for a while'. Only when the material had attained a 'presence' for the artist would it be exhibited.[12] Within this logic of ineffable accreted value, the corner positioning of *Pieces* takes on a coy resonance. As the impoverished material is transposed to the gallery, the passing of this threshold affords the work its 'presence', and by extension the attainment of value by the inherently valueless. Parsons' enigmatic statement that this transubstantiation had occurred at a previous stage, foregrounds a temporal discrepancy as a point of crisis: the social rupture in the dislocation of value from conditions of material and labour. The

---

In allen drei Fällen wechselte die Figur der Ecke in ihrer materiellen Präsenz: vom Sujet des Holzschnitts zum Bestandteil des Materials bei *Apples* und zur strukturellen Stütze bei *Corner Seat*. Als operative Form rahmte sie materiell wie symbolisch eine Reihe von Aktionen in den Bereichen künstlerischer Produktion und Rezeption, die implizit um die entgegengesetzten Ebenen Arbeit und Passivität, Bewerten und Entwerten strukturiert schienen. So besaß der Holzschnitt als handwerkliche Form, die emblematisch für einen anachronistischen physischen Prozess steht und als solche kritisch unterlaufen wird, durch seine mühevolle Produktion einer ikonographischen Abstraktion andächtige Eigenschaften; die Eckbank als relativ passive künstlerische Geste fasste die kontemplative Betrachtung als unbehagliche Parallele zum kritischen Urteil, und *Apples* stellte die Entscheidung des Betrachters zu einer Transaktion – einen Apfel nehmen oder nicht – ins Zentrum seines produktiven Potentials. In diese Aktionen gingen die symbolische Grundlage der Ecke, ihre Assoziation mit Verlegenheit und Scham, als soziale Formen des Urteils ein – die veränderliche Bewertung des Werks und seiner Grundlage in einer verschränkten Beziehung zu einer etablierten Ordnung der Kritik.

Das Archivbild von Laurie Parsons *Pieces* zeigt das Werk in einer Ecke, die von einer Treppe definiert ist. Diese merkwürdige Anordnung verweist auf die bewusste Entscheidung, es an einer Schwelle jenseits des konventionellen Bereichs eines Ausstellungsraumes zu verorten. Die Objekte, aus denen sich *Pieces* zusammensetzt, sind eindeutig aus den Gebrauchs- und Tauschsystemen herausgefallen, ihre auffällige Entwertung erhöht die Bedeutung des kontextuellen Wechsels zwischen der „realen" Welt und dem Kunstmuseum und betont die Kontingenz der Definition von „Material" in Bezug auf diese Strukturen.

HAP Grieshaber / Franz Fühmann: Engel der Geschichte 25: Engel der Behinderten, Classen Verlag Düsseldorf 1982, (HAP Grieshaber / Franz Fühmann: Angel of History 25: Angel of the Disabled), 2010

corner location is completely in keeping with the abject materiality of the work's constituent parts, yet within their new framework of apprehension these associations become theatrical. The context of the art gallery defines the action of the viewer towards the artwork – to 'invest' in it as an abstraction, in relation to its surroundings and its potential to communicate meaning – whereas the material constitution of *Pieces* and the implications of its physical siting appeal to notions of impoverishment and reticence; to that which falls below expectation. This friction between the gestures of showing and withdrawal, the circulation of value and the affective associations of the devalued, emphasizes the social imaginary around the artwork's material foundations as a facet of ethical and critical judgement.

Andrea Büttner's citing of the hagiography of St. Francis of Assisi through the title of her exhibitions in London and Reggio Emilia, is echoed in works from the preceding four years, including woodcuts of scenes from the *Fioretti di St Francesco d'Assisi*, the collection of popular legends about the saint.[13] A leitmotif that Büttner has adopted in her representation of St. Francis, and paralleled in non-figurative works, is the symbolism of fabric in his biography and the subsequent iconography of material in the Franciscan order. The saint came from a wealthy background established by his father's work as a cloth trader. Francis' disavowal of this wealth is marked by the story of his disrobing in front of his father, the 'renouncing [of] his patrimony' symbolized by the rejection of his fine clothing.[14] The Catholic Church now sanctifies soiled tunics Francis is said to have subsequently worn as religious relics – they have come to represent the saint's wilful poverty as an investment in spiritual treasures to come.

In Parsons Prozess des Sammelns und Präsentierens von „Dingen" gab es eine Übergangsphase, in der sie die Objekte in ihrem Atelier aufbewahrte und „eine Weile mit ihnen lebte." Erst wenn das Material für die Künstlerin eine „Präsenz" bekommen hatte, wurde es ausgestellt.[12] In der Positionierung von *Pieces* in der Ecke klingt diese Logik des unbegreiflicherweise angesammelten Werts auf verschämte Weise an. Aus der Verlagerung dieses ärmlichen Materials in die Ausstellung bezieht das Werk beim Überschreiten der Schwelle seine „Präsenz" und das inhärent Wertlose wird wertvoll. Parsons enigmatische Äußerung, dass sich diese Transsubstantiation in einem früheren Stadium vollzogen habe, rückt die zeitliche Diskrepanz als Krisenpunkt in den Vordergrund: den sozialen Bruch durch die Dislozierung des Werts von den Bedingungen des Materials und der Arbeit. Der Ort des Werks in der Ecke deckt sich völlig mit der erbärmlichen Materialität seiner Bestandteile, aber dennoch lässt der neue Bezugsrahmen diese Assoziationen theatralisch wirken. Der Kontext des Kunstmuseums definiert das Verhalten des Betrachters gegenüber dem Kunstwerk - er „investiert" in seine Abstraktion in Hinblick auf seine Umgebung und sein Potential, Bedeutung zu kommunizieren – während die materiellen Bestandteile von *Pieces* und sein physischer Standort Begriffe wie Verarmung und Rückzug evozieren, Vorstellungen von dem, was hinter den Erwartungen zurückbleibt. Diese Reibung zwischen Ausstellung und Rückzug, zwischen der Zirkulation von Wert und von affektiven Assoziationen des Ent-Werteten unterstreichen die soziale Bildsprache der materiellen Grundlagen des Kunstwerks als Facette eines ethischen und kritischen Urteils.

Andrea Büttners Verweis auf die Hagiographie des heiligen Franziskus im Titel ihrer Ausstellungen in London und Reggio Emilia

In *The Poverty of Riches*, Büttner displayed a grid of photographs
on a table covered in dark red cloth (*Table*, 2011). At one corner
of this grid, a postcard image showed the relic of St. Francis'
tunic on view in Assisi. A combination of photographs taken
by the artist, and a number of found reproductions of artworks,
the images on the table constituted a network of formal and
contextual associations emanating from the relic's material and
symbolic status. The relations between the images formed a
microcosm of those within the broader scope of the exhibition,
reflecting on the processes of research and production undertaken
by Büttner.

Next to the tunic postcard a photograph of an Alberto Burri painting, composed of stitched hessian sections, formed a direct visual
connection to the dishevelled patchwork of the habit of St. Francis.
The proto-Arte Povera of Burri's work was mirrored in images of
a Pierro Manzoni painting – a white 'achrome' grid – and a later
Mario Merz installation of fruit on a glass table (*La frutta siamo noi*,
1988), all of which form part of the Maramotti Collection. This
reflexivity towards the circumstances of the exhibition extended
to photographs that loosely served as documents of Büttner's
preceding residency in Italy, and time spent as a guest of religious
communities in the region: a snapshot of stacked Monobloc chairs
in a church, a photograph of Leonardo's *The Last Supper* partially
obscured by the heads of viewers, the clothed surface of a church
altar, a modestly laid table and chairs (again, Monobloc) on a
terrace overlooking Umbrian hills, the artist's stretched-out legs on
a sparse tiled floor, a gridded Ikea-style storage unit in the same
room, holding coloured yarns.

Within the allegorical narrative of St. Francis' poverty, his brown
robes were formed from stitched-together sections of un-dyed

findet sich in anderer Form auch in Werken aus den vorangegangenen vier Jahren, zum Beispiel in Holzschnitten mit Szenen aus
der Sammlung volkstümlicher Legenden über den Heiligen, den
Fioretti di San Francesco d'Assisi.[13] Ein Leitmotiv, das Büttner in ihrer
Darstellung des Heiligen Franziskus übernommen und für das
sie in nicht-figurativen Werken Entsprechungen gefunden hat, ist
der Symbolismus von Stoff in seiner Biographie und in der anschlie-
ßenden Ikonographie des Franziskanerordens. Die Familie des
Heiligen verdankte ihren Reichtum der Arbeit des Vaters als Stoff-
händler; für die Zurückweisung dieses Reichtums steht die Geschichte, wonach er sich vor dem Vater entkleidet habe – die Rück-
gabe der schönen Kleidung symbolisiert also das „Ausschlagen
des väterlichen Erbes".[14] Die katholische Kirche betrachtet die
beschmutzten Kutten, die Franziskus danach angeblich getragen
hat, als Reliquien, nun die freiwillige Armut des Heiligen als Investition in künftige spirituelle Schätze sie repräsentieren.

In *The Poverty of Riches* gab es ein Raster aus Fotos auf einem mit
dunkelrotem Tuch bedeckten Tisch (*Table,* 2011). An der einen
Ecke lag eine Ansichtskarte mit dem Bild der Reste einer Kutte
des Heiligen Franziskus, die in Assisi ausgestellt ist. Die Kom-
bination aus eigenen Fotos der Künstlerin und Reproduktionen
von Kunstwerken bildete ein Netz aus formalen und kontextuellen Assoziationen, die sich aus dem Material und dem symbolischen Status der Reliquie ergaben. Die Beziehungen zwischen
den Bildern entsprachen im Kleinen den Werken in der übrigen
Ausstellung und reflektierten Büttners Forschungs- und Produkti-
onsprozesse.

Das neben der Postkarte mit der Kutte liegende Foto eines Werks
von Alberto Burri, das aus zusammengehefteten Abschnitten
aus Sackleinen bestand, stellte eine direkte visuelle Verbindung

cloth given to him by the poor of Assisi. The brown habit has consequently become a cipher for the vows of poverty taken by the Franciscan order, while also connoting earthy baseness. Büttner's paralleling of 'holy' poverty with the impoverished materiality of proto-Arte Povera emphasizes the dual, ethical movements in these positions. As Burri and Manzoni sought to use the basic material of painting – its fabric support – as a performative medium to articulate the debasing and disruption of an established aesthetic and social order, the dishevelled relic of St. Francis exists as a psychoanalytically charged symbol of physical abjection as social dissent – not unlike the 'shit-space' Büttner has previously created as a context for her exhibitions, by painting the gallery walls brown.[15] However, the performativity of fabric is also highlighted in relation to notions of purity; the white, seamed grid of Manzoni's 'achrome' is a motif that reappears in the folded tablecloth of *The Last Supper*, the altar cloth, and, more obliquely, the patterning on the Monobloc chairs. But whereas the 'pure' modernist grid asserts the displacement of the dimensions and objects of the real by 'the lateral spread of a single surface', and in so doing implicates a 'staircase to the Universal', Büttner, in an extrapolation of Manzoni's fabric folds, emphasizes the grid as symptom of quotidian, serial materiality.[16] At a juncture between the material and the spiritual the collation of images echoes Rosalind Krauss' statement: 'by now we find it indescribably embarrassing to mention *art* and *spirit* in the same sentence... The peculiar power of the grid... arises from its potential to preside over this shame: to mask and reveal it at one and the same time.'[17]
Underpinning the principles of both Arte Povera and the Franciscan religious order is the adoption of material poverty as strategy. In his publication *The Poverty of Riches: St Francis of Assisi*

zu dem zerfetzten Patchwork des Habits des Heiligen her. Burris Proto-Arte-Povera-Stil spiegelte sich in Reproduktionen eines Gemäldes von Piero Manzoni – ein weißes „Achrome" – und einer späteren Installation von Früchten auf einem Glastisch von Mario Merz (*La Frutta siamo noi*, 1988). Beide Werke sind Teil der Sammlung Maramotti. Dieser Rückbezug auf die Umstände der Ausstellung erstreckte sich auch auf Fotos, die Büttners vorangegangenen Aufenthalt in Italien und ihre Zeit als Gast in Klöstern der Region dokumentierten: ein Schnappschuss von einem Stapel Monobloc-Stühle in einer Kirche, ein Foto von Leonardos *Letztem Abendmahl*, teilweise durch die Köpfe der Betrachter verdeckt, ein mit Stoff bedeckter Altar, ein bescheiden gedeckter Tisch und Stühle (wieder Monobloc) auf einer Terrasse mit Blick auf die umbrischen Hügel, die ausgestreckten Beine der Künstlerin auf einem kargen, gefliesten Boden, eine gerasterte Regalwand im Ikea-Stil, gefüllt mit farbigen Garnen, im selben Raum.
In der allegorischen Erzählung über die Armut des Heiligen bestand seine braune Kutte aus zusammengenähten, ungefärbten Stoffstücken, die ihm die Armen in Assisi gegeben hatten. Der braune Habit wurde zur Chiffre für das Armutsgelübde der Franziskaner, ist aber gleichzeitig auch mit irdischer Niedrigkeit konnotiert. Büttners Parallelisierung der „heiligen" Armut mit der ärmlichen Materialität der Proto-Arte Povera betont die Dualität der ethischen Bewegungen in diesen Positionen. Während Burri und Manzoni die Materialien der Malerei – ihre stoffliche Grundlage – als performatives Medium zur Artikulation der Entwertung und Zerstörung einer etablierten ästhetischen und gesellschaftlichen Ordnung nutzten, sind die zerfetzten Reliquien des Heiligen Franziskus ein psychoanalytisch besetztes Symbol für die physische Abjektion als sozialem Dissent – nicht unähnlich dem *shit-space*, den Büttner

Fallen lassen (letting fall), 2010

Before carrying out any of the other instructions, take your jacket off and hang it somewhere in the space for the duration of the exhibition. (David Raymond Conroy)

Write down a dialogue that meant something to you recently. You can then alter the sheet of paper in any way you want, but you are not allowed to take it out of the room. (Leonie Weber)

Reconsidered Baxter Wolf discusses St. Francis' 'divestment' from
this world as an 'investment' in the next, a 'spiritually beneficial,
socially powerful kind of poverty' that was not open to the
'true' poor of Assisi.[18] This paradox of a privileged state of poverty
emphasizes the act of exposure; how such divestment is revealed
and performed to the world. It forms a necessary contradiction
in its relations to the involuntary poor, whereby the impoverished
Francis lowers himself to a state of shared destitution, while being
held in a state of otherness defined by his spiritual quest. A tension exists between withdrawal as a function of personal spiritual
attainment, investment in the spectacle of exposure as a means
of rousing a sense of moral duty in others, and an active life of service to the spiritual and physical needs of others.
The final photograph on Büttner's *Table* showed gridded shelving
and stacks of yarn for weaving, and spoke of a space of intensive
domestic work. Within the wider scope of the artist's practice,
the image equates to a series of photographs, objects and videos
stemming from her time spent with groups of nuns. These works
have specifically addressed forms of labour, both creative and
more mundane, undertaken by the nuns as acts of giving service
and thanks for 'God-given' talents. This notion of work is marked
by humbleness, in the modest display of creative gifts through
amateur craft, or through menial material tasks. What is most
redolent in these actions is the coupling of an affirmative move
towards poverty as spiritual progress, with an affective tension
between exposure and withdrawal. As fabric in religious narratives
'performs' the acts of covering and becoming naked as contingent
heuristics, so within the logic of production the move towards
'littleness' is coupled with the paradoxical desire to invoke
accomplishment as an engine of reciprocity. In the words of a Little

zuvor als Kontext für ihre Ausstellung geschaffen hat, indem sie
eine Galeriewand braun anmalte.[15] Die Performativität von
Stoff wird aber auch in Beziehung zu Reinheitsbegriffen gesetzt:
das Motiv des weißen, zerfurchten Rasters in Manzonis *Achrome*
kehrt in dem gefalteten Tischtuch des *Letzten Abendmahls*, der
Altardecke und, weniger deutlich, in der Musterung der Monobloc-
Stühle wieder. Aber während das „reine" modernistische Raster
die Verschiebung der Dimensionen und Objekte des Realen durch
„die seitliche Ausbreitung einer einzigen Fläche" behauptet und
damit eine „Treppe zum Allgemeinen" impliziert[16], betont Büttner
das Raster als Symptom alltäglicher, serieller Materialität. An
der Schnittstelle zwischen dem Materiellen und dem Spirituellen
wiederholt ihre Zusammenstellung der Bilder die Bemerkung von
Rosalind Krauss, dass „wir es heute als unbeschreiblich peinlich
empfinden, wenn *Kunst* und *Spiritualität* im gleichen Satz erwähnt
werden. Die eigentümliche Macht des Rasters [...] entspringt seinem
Vermögen, dieses Gefühl der Scham zu kontrollieren, es gleichzeitig zu verschleiern und zu enthüllen".[17]
Eine Grundlage der Prinzipien der Arte Povera und des Franziskanerordens ist die Aneignung materieller Armut als Strategie.
In seinem Buch *The Poverty of Riches: St Francis of Assisi Reconsidered*
diskutiert Baxter Wolf die „Entkleidung" des Heiligen „von seiner
Welt" als „Investition' in die nächste", als „spirituell vorteilhafte,
gesellschaftlich mächtige Form der Armut", die den „echten" Armen
von Assisi nicht offen stand.[18] Dieses Paradox eines privilegierten
Zustands der Armut betont den Akt der Darstellung: die Form, in
der diese Entkleidung der Welt offenbart und vorgeführt wird. Es
ist ein notwendiger Widerspruch in seiner Beziehung zu den un-
freiwillig Armen, wenn sich der verarmte Franziskus im gemeinsamen
Elend erniedrigt, während er durch seine spirituelle Suche der

Fallen lassen (letting fall), 2010
Put a carrot and two pieces of charcoal on the floor. The title could be
Remnants of a snowman. (Katharina Hacker)

Sister interviewed by Büttner:
'I like to make little works in an artistic sense, I don't want to
say "oh I can't see beauty, I don't know anything", no, I have gifts
given to me by the Lord so that these gifts are able to serve others.
"Littleness" doesn't mean I don't have anything... but what I have
I received from God. It's not mine, its something I've received and
that I share with others.'[19]

Two years after producing *Pieces*, for a solo exhibition at the
Forum Kunst Rottweil, Laurie Parsons moved into the gallery for
seven weeks, while working in a local psychiatric hospital and a
school for disabled children.[20] She kept the gallery doors unlocked
day and night, welcoming visits from local people who came to
talk with her. This commandeering of the gallery for unmediated
social interaction was emphasized in the wording of the exhibition
announcement, in which Parsons included her name alongside
that of the curator, and the people of Rottweil. As a development
from, rather than reaction against her earlier object-based works,
her actions can be seen as ones of deliberate self-impoverishment.
The work divests the gallery space of physical display, through
the reduction of the material of the artwork to the social relations
between artist and public. Parsons' positioning of herself in
lieu of an 'exhibition' amounts to passivity – a non-prescriptive
engagement with the people of Rottweil, as a substitute for
material production to which value can be attributed – and a
conscious marking of the gallery as a space of exposure through
'exhibiting' her life, and through the displacement of any
object of judgement. In these last vestiges of Parsons' use of a
gallery space in her practice the consideration of the critical 'value'
of an artwork is projected outwards towards a more direct proc-

Andere bleibt. Es gibt eine Spannung zwischen dem Rückzug um
des persönlichen spirituellen Gewinns willen, dem Spektakel als
Weckruf zur moralischen Pflicht und dem Leben im Dienst der
spirituellen und physischen Bedürfnisse anderer.
Das letzte Foto auf Büttners *Table* zeigte gerasterte Regale mit
gestapeltem Garn für die Weberei, die von einem Raum intensiver
häuslicher Arbeit sprachen. Im Rahmen ihrer künstlerischen Praxis
entspricht das Bild einer Serie von Fotos, Objekten und Videos
aus der Zeit, die sie mit Gruppen von Nonnen verbrachte; Werke,
die sich spezifisch mit Formen kreativer, aber auch alltäglicher
Arbeit beschäftigen, die die Nonnen als Akte des Gottesdienstes
und des Dankes für „gottgegebene" Talente verstehen. Das Kenn-
zeichen dieses Arbeitsbegriffs ist die Demut, sei es in bescheidenen
kreativen Amateur-Handarbeiten oder in dienenden materiellen
Tätigkeiten. Auffallend in diesem Zusammenhang ist die Verbindung einer affirmativen Bewegung hin zur Armut als spirituellem
Fortschritt mit einer affektiven Spannung zwischen Darstellung
und Rückzug. So wie der Stoff in religiösen Legenden die Akte des
Bedeckens und Entkleidens als heuristische Kontingenz „zeigt",
so paart sich der Schritt zum „Kleinen" innerhalb der Logik der
Produktion mit dem paradoxen Begehren, Verrichtungen als Motor
der Gegenseitigkeit zu begreifen. Mit den Worten einer Kleinen
Schwester Jesu im Interview mit Büttner: „Ich mache gerne Kleine
Werke im künstlerischen Sinne; ich will nicht sagen: ‚Oh, ich kann
Schönheit nicht sehen, ich weiß nichts', nein, Gott hat mir Gaben
gegeben, damit diese Gaben anderen dienen können. ‚Klein ' heißt
nicht, dass ich nichts habe... aber was ich habe, habe ich von
Gott empfangen. Es gehört mir nicht, es ist etwas, das ich empfangen habe und mit anderen teile."[19]

Fallen lassen (letting fall), 2010

Take a bag, ideally a boxing bag, fill it with sand and put a hole in it, so that
the sand trickles out. (Sandra Kranich)

Let a leaf fall down. (Dick Jewell)

ess of personal compromise and moral valuation; that of work as 'social giving'.

On a number of occasions Andrea Büttner has exhibited a series of eight Xeroxed photographs titled *HAP Grieshaber/Franz Fühmann, Engel der Geschichte 25: Engel der Behinderten, Classen Verlag Düsseldorf 1982*. The images are taken directly from *Angel of the Disabled*, the twenty-fifth issue of the magazine *Angel of History* produced by the German artist HAP Grieshaber.[21] The black and white photographs, scaled up and exhibited by Büttner in clip frames, show an exhibition of Grieshaber's woodcut series *Totentanz von Basel* in two homes for teenagers with learning disabilities – groups of young men are shown viewing the works. While Büttner originally presented these extracted images alongside an exhibition of Grieshaber's magazines curated by her in 2010, she has subsequently shown them independently, relatively detached from reference to their original context.[22] This gesture isolates the images' concentration on capturing the reactions of the teenage viewers to the exhibition, the conspicuous openness of their expressions of interest and contemplation. For the viewer of the re-presented images a doubling occurs: a reflexivity towards one's own position as a viewer of an artwork, and an observer of the teenagers' equivalent experience. Embedded in this self-awareness is the realization of a perceived disparity in judgement – a presumptuous characterization of Grieshaber's audience as displaying vulnerability in their receptivity, as opposed to the supposedly authoritative critical address of a contemporary art audience. This realization is jarring, and coupled with Büttner's own position as artist in relation to Grieshaber's images – one of passive transposition, rather than authored production – the presentational gesture suggests the affirmation of an affectively loaded movement, an

Zwei Jahre nach der Fertigstellung von *Pieces* zog Laurie Parsons für eine Einzelausstellung sieben Wochen lang ins Forum Kunst Rottweil[20] ein. Sie arbeitete in dieser Zeit in einer Psychiatrie und an einer Schule für behinderte Kinder. Die Türen der Galerie waren Tag und Nacht geöffnet und sie empfing Besucher aus dem Ort, die sich mit ihr unterhalten wollten. Ihre Aneignung dieses Raums für so unvermittelte soziale Interaktion wurde durch die Ankündigung der Ausstellung unterstrichen, in der Parsons ihren Namen neben dem des Kurators und der Bürger von Rottweil aufführte. Ihre Aktionen, die ihre früheren, objektbasierten Arbeiten weiterentwickelten und nicht nur darauf reagierten, lassen sich als bewusste Selbstverarmung verstehen. Durch die Reduktion des künstlerischen Materials auf die sozialen Beziehungen zwischen Künstlerin und Öffentlichkeit entkleidet sie den Ausstellungsraum seiner physischen Ausstellungsgegenstände. Dass Parsons sich selbst an die Stelle einer „Ausstellung" setzt, läuft auf Passivität hinaus – auf eine unvorschriftsmäßige Beschäftigung mit den Rottweiler Bürgern als Ersatz für eine valorisierbare materielle Produktion – und indem sie sich selbst und ihr Leben „ausstellt" und jedes Objekt, das beurteilt werden könnte, vermeidet, markiert sie den Ausstellungsraum bewusst als Ort des Ausgesetztseins. In diesen letzten Spuren der Nutzung des Ausstellungsraums liegt der kritische „Wert" eines Kunstwerks außerhalb dieses Raumes, in einem unmittelbareren Ort persönlicher Kompromisse und moralischer Bewertung: das Werk wird zur „sozialen Hingabe".

Andrea Büttner hat bei mehreren Gelegenheiten eine Serie von acht fotokopierten Fotos mit dem Titel *HAP Grieshaber/Franz Fühmann, Engel der Geschichte 25: Engel der Behinderten,* Classen Verlag, Düsseldorf 1982, gezeigt. Die Bilder sind der 25. Ausgabe der Zeitschrift *Engel der Geschichte* des deutschen Künstlers

Fallen lassen (letting fall), 2010

Play 'cat's cradle', and when you have finished, leave the string on the floor. (Anthony Auerbach)

Place a plastic cup full of water on the floor. (Hugo Canoilas)

'open devotion', that is dialectically entwined with, as opposed to reactionary against, critical judgement.[23]

Laurie Parsons' investigations as an artist into the material and social sphere of the institution of art, led to her eventual dismissal of this arena of production and reception. Existing across seven years of gallery-based practice were forms of material and symbolic equivalence that simultaneously illuminated and displaced forms of value, while asserting a social desire, an affectively motivated movement towards 'giving'. Andrea Büttner's work evokes the crisis within this movement less as a *via negativa*, than as a heuristic experience of vulnerability as written into artwork, and as an affirmative speculation on critical judgement beyond the production of value within social relations. Her precisely gauged presentations of crafted objects and prints, found materials, reflexive gestures and documentary media amount to a dialectical investment in the artwork as both material thing and epistemic structure. As a vector within these states, poverty as methodology and allegory exists to position privilege, while paradoxically positing receptivity outside of the retentiveness of rationality. The notion of 'open devotion' as the conjunctive of emotional stirring and the exercising of social faculty, is for Büttner crucially linked to the 'implicit knowledge of the emotional and physical elements' of art.[24]

1

The artwork came to be in the collection of the museum through its joint acquisition of the Ricke Collection, with the Kunstmuseum St. Gallen and the Kunstmuseum Liechenstein, in 2007. From the 1960s to the 1990s Rolf Ricke's Cologne gallery was the location of the first European exhibitions for a number of key US artists, the gallery's focus stemming from a lineage of minimal, post-minimal and conceptual practices. In 1989 he presented Laurie Parsons' work for the first time outside New York.

2

See the museum's website: http://www. mmk-frankfurt.de/en/sammlung/werkdeta ilseite/?werk=2006%2F248 .

3

Bob Nickas, 'Dematerial Girl', *Artforum*, April 2003.

HAP Grieshaber entnommen.[21] Die Schwarzweiß-Fotografien, die Büttner vergrößert und gerahmt hat, zeigen Gruppen von jungen Männern bei der Betrachtung einer Ausstellung von Grieshabers Holzschnitt-Serie *Totentanz von Basel* in zwei Heimen für geistig Behinderte. Büttner hat diese Bilder ursprünglich im Rahmen einer 2010 von ihr kuratierten Ausstellung zu Grieshabers Zeitschriften gezeigt[22], sie seither aber auch in anderen Zusammenhängen ausgestellt, aus ihrem ursprünglichen Kontext gelöst, so dass sie auf die Reaktion der jugendlichen Betrachter der Ausstellung, auf ihr auffallend offenes Interesse und ihre Kontemplation fokussiert wurden. Der Betrachter der erneut präsentierten Bilder erlebt eine Doppelung: die Reflexion über die eigene Person als Betrachter eines Kunstwerks und als Beobachter der entsprechenden Erfahrung der Jugendlichen. Eingebettet in diese Selbst-Bewusstheit ist die Erkenntnis einer Disparität des Urteils – die vermessene Charakterisierung von Grieshabers Publikum als durch seine Empfänglichkeit verletzbar steht im Gegensatz zu dem vermeintlich autoritativen Anspruch eines zeitgenössischen Kunstpublikums. Diese Erkenntnis irritiert, und der Gestus der Präsentation verweist, gepaart mit Büttners eigener Position als Künstlerin gegenüber Grieshabers Bildern – passive Umkehrung statt eigener Produktion – auf die Affirmation einer affektiv besetzten Bewegtheit, einer „Rührungsfähigkeit"[23], die kritisches Urteil nicht negiert, sondern sich mit ihm dialektisch verschränkt.

Laurie Parsons künstlerische Untersuchung der materiellen und sozialen Sphäre der Institution Kunst führte schließlich dazu, dass sie diese Arena der Produktion und Rezeption aufgab. In den sieben Jahren ihrer Ausstellungstätigkeit entstanden Formen materieller und symbolischer Äquivalenz, die Formen des Werts gleichzeitig beleuchteten und verschoben, während sie ein soziales

Fallen lassen (letting fall), 2010

Leave something purposefully unaltered in the space. (Hannah Rickards)

Let a helium filled tiger balloon rise. During the length of the exhibition it will fall. (Andrea Büttner)

4

Lorence-Monk Gallery, New York, 1990.

5

Ibid.

6

The work was included in *The Big Nothing*, New Museum, New York, 1992.

7

Laurie Parsons, *Security and Admissions Project*, as part of 'The Spatial Drive', New Museum, New York, 1992.

8

Martin Beck, 'Design and Museums', *Critical Condition*, Kokerei Zollverein, Essen, 2003, pp. 333–5.

9

Kenneth Baxter Wolf, *The Poverty of Riches: St Francis of Assisi Reconsidered*, Oxford University Press, Oxford, 2003.

10

An example would be *Dancing Nuns; A stone Schwitters painted in the Lake District; L, M, A* (2008), a photographic screen print in which the artist and her gallerists hide under a piece of cloth

11

Büttner's 2010 performative work *Fallen Lassen* (letting fall) was literally based around gestures that displayed an 'affirmative attitude' to falling.

12

Nickas, op. cit.

13

'The Little Flowers of St Francis of Assisi', available online at http://www.ewtn.com/library/mary/flowers.htm (accessed 3 February 2013).

14

Baxter Wolf, op. cit., p. 4.

15

For a more developed discussion of Büttner's 'shit-space' see Richard Birkett, 'Andrea Büttner: The Shame of Culture', *MAP*, Issue 23, p. 46.

16

Rosalind E. Krauss, *The Originality of the Avant-Garde and Other Modernist Myths*, MIT Press, Boston, MA, 1986, p. 10.

17

Ibid. p. 12.

18

Baxter Wolf, op. cit., p. 4.

19

Andrea Büttner, *Little Sisters: Lunapark Ostia*, 2012, HD video, 42 min.

20

Curated by Udo Kittelmann.

21

HAP Grieshaber/Franz Fühmann, *Engel der Geschichte 25: Engel der Behinderten*, Classen Verlag Düsseldorf, 1982.

22

HAP Grieshaber: Der Engel der Geschichte (The Angel of History), 1964–1981, Hollybush Gardens, London, 2010.

23

From the Grimm's Dictionary definition of 'RÜHRUNGSFÄHIGKEIT', a phrase used by Friedrich Schiller in a letter to Johann Wolfgang von Goethe. Quoted by Andrea Büttner in Andrea Büttner and Isla Leaver-Yap, 'Re: Andacht zum kleinen', *The Assistants*, Fiona Meade, ed., Mousse Publishing, Milan, 2013, p. 32

24

Büttner and Leaver-Yap, op. cit., p. 32.

Begehren, eine affektiv motivierte Bewegung in Richtung auf „Hingabe" geltend machten. Andrea Büttners Werk evoziert die Krise in dieser Bewegung weniger als *via negativa* denn als eine dem Kunstwerk eingeschriebene heuristische Erfahrung von Verletzbarkeit und als affirmative Spekulation über das kritische Urteil jenseits der Wertproduktion in sozialen Beziehungen.

Ihre exakt eingesetzten Präsentationen von handgemachten Objekten und Drucken, gefundenen Materialien, reflexiven Gesten und dokumentarischen Medien verweisen auf eine dialektische Besetzung des Kunstwerks als gleichzeitig materielles Ding und epistemische Struktur. Ein Vektor darin ist die Armut als Methode und Allegorie, die Privilegiertheit verortet, paradoxerweise aber auch die Rezeptivität jenseits des Puffers der Rationalität positioniert. Der Begriff der „Rührungsfähigkeit" als Verbindung von emotionaler Rührung und Ausübung sozialer Fähigkeit ist für Büttner wesentlich an die „implizite Kenntnis der emotionalen und physischen Elemente"[24] der Kunst geknüpft.

1

Ehemalige Sammlung Rolf Ricke im MMK Museum für Moderne Kunst Frankfurt am Main, Kunstmuseum, St. Gallen und Kunstmuseum Liechtenstein, Vaduz. Von den 1960er bis in die 1990 Jahre zeigt Rolf Rickes Kölner Galerie als erste die wichtigsten US-Künstler; ihr Fokus entwickelte sich aus der minimalistischen, post-minimalistischen und konzeptuellen Tradition. 1989 zeigte Ricke Laurie Parsons Werke erstmals außerhalb von New York.

2

http://www.mmk-frankfurt.de/de/sammlung/werkdetailseite/?werk=2006%2F248 (16. Februar 2013).

3

Bob Nickas, „Demateral Girl", Artforum April 2003.

4

Lorence-Monk Gallery, New York 1990.

5

Ebd.

6

Das Werk wurde in der Ausstellung *The Big Nothing* gezeigt, New Museum, New York 1992.

7

Laurie Parsons, *Security and Admissions Project*, Teil der Ausstellung *The Spatial Drive*, New Museum, New York 1992.

8

Martin Beck, „Design and Museums", Critical Condition, Kokerei Zollverein 2003, S. 333-335.

Fallen lassen (letting fall), 2010

Find a *gestalt* for defenselessness: pick the spikes off a cactus and leave them beside the plant. (Malin Ståhl)

9
Kenneth Baxter Wolf, The Power of Riches: St. Francis of Assisi Reconsidered. Oxford 2003.

10
Ein Beispiel wäre *Dancing Nuns; A stone Schwitters painted in the Lake District; L, M, A* (2008), ein Foto-Siebdruck, in dem die Künstlerin und ihre Galeristin sich unter einem Stück Stoff verstecken.

11
Büttners performative Arbeit *Fallen lassen* basierte im Wortsinn auf Gesten, die eine „affirmative Einstellung" zum Fallen zeigten.

12
Nickas, "Dematerial Girl"

13
„The Little Flowers of St. Francis of Assisi", http://www.ewtn.com/library/mary/flowers.htm (3. Februar 2013).

14
Kenneth Baxter Wolf, *The Poverty of Riches*, S. 4.

15
Eine ausführlichere Diskussion über Büttners *shit space* bei Richard Birkett, „Andrea Büttner: The Shame of Culture", MAP, 23, S. 46.

16
Rosalind E. Krauss, Die Originalität der Avantgarde und andere Mythen der Moderne. Aus d. Amerikanischen von Jörg Heininger. Amsterdam/Dresden 2000, S. 51-53.

17
Ebd., S. 55.

18
Kenneth Baxter Wolf, The Poverty of Riches, S. 4.

19
Andrea Büttner, *Little Sisters: Lunapark Ostia*, 2012, HD-Video, 42 Min.

20
Kuratiert von Udo Kittelmann.

21
HAP Grieshaber/Franz Fühmann, *Engel der Geschichte 25: Engel der Behinderten*, Classen Verlag, Düsseldorf 1982.

22
HAP Grieshaber: Der Engel der Geschichte (The Angel of History), 1964-1981, Hollybush Gardens, London 2010.

23
Vgl. Grimms Wörterbuch. Den Begriff der Rührungsfähigkeit hat Friedrich Schiller in einem Brief an Johann Wolfgang von Goethe benutzt. Andrea Büttner zitiert ihn in Andrea Büttner und Isla Leaver-Yap, 'Re: Andacht zum kleinen', *The Assistants*, Ed. Fionn Meade, Mousse Publishing, Mailand, 2013, S. 32

24
Büttner and Leaver-Yap, op. cit., S. 32.

Fallen lassen (letting fall), 2010

Take a glass object that is dear to you, wrap it in clear tape and balance it on your head. It will fall and the cracks will indicate your height. Then you can let go of the fear of ever letting it fall again. (Michael Dean)

Clay Sculpture, 2010, unfired clay, 30 × 390 × 30 cm, 500 kg.
Installation view, Raven Row.

Ahnenknödel (ancestor dumplings), 2009, unfired clay, water, plastic, dimensions variable. Installation view, Hollybush Gardens.

Diamantenstuhl (diamond chair), 2011, rough brown diamond,
Monobloc chair, 77 x 55 x 55 cm. Installation view, Artpace.

Diamantenstuhl (diamond chair), detail, 2011

ATM, 2011, digital pigment print, 40 × 60 cm

Fountain, 2011, unfired clay, pumps, basins, water, 81.3 × 95.3 × 95.3 cm.
Installation view, Artpace.

Untitled (bronze shelf), 2012, cast bronze, 6 × 11 × 7 cm

Untitled (cardboard object on bronze shelf), 2012, cardboard house won
at Lunapark Ostia and cast bronze shelf, 19 x 21 x 15 cm.
Installation view, *Documenta 13*.

THERE ARE NO IDEAS, EXCEPT IN THE THINGS THEMSELVES
Chus Martinez

One of the main difficulties with writing about a work of art arises when one needs to engage with its description. It is best to keep it simple. Andrea Büttner works with many different materials and mediums: there are woodcuts, normally large scale, small glass paintings, video works, objects, sometimes combined with found objects, and she also uses found photographs, slides, and, lately, moss.

At first impression, it seems that all of the work deals with a certain condition that is linked to the Catholic faith. However, it would be misleading to state that Büttner's work has a subject and is revolving around a theme or way of thinking related to this religion, or to poverty, for example. In actual fact, the work is not *about* anything. It does not produce a set of references to a tradition or a set of moral and aesthetical values. It actually emerges *from* them. It is difficult to isolate one particular woodcut, glass painting or video piece, and to understand the ambition behind the work. At the same time, it would be wrong to suggest that a group of works might constitute an 'installation'. Büttner's works do not primarily respond to the space around them, even if they obviously relate to it. It is easy to focus on one piece in particular, but the individual works make sense only in relationship to others. Each piece has a dialogical relationship with the totality of the artist's practice. In other words, the function of every single work is not to illustrate a subject, but to orient us towards a problem that resonates throughout Büttner's oeuvre: how to make us think about a new life.

ES GIBT KEINE IDEEN AUSSERHALB DER DINGE
Chus Martinez

Das größte Problem beim Schreiben über ein Kunstwerk liegt in der Beschreibung. Hier ist Einfachheit am besten. Andrea Büttner arbeitet mit vielen verschiedenen Materialien und Medien: Holzschnitte, meist großformatig, kleine Glasmalereien, Videos, Objekte, gelegentlich kombiniert mit gefundenen Objekten und Fotos, Dias und seit kurzem auch mit Moos.

Auf den ersten Blick scheint es, als beschäftige sich das gesamte Werk mit einem bestimmten Zustand, der mit der katholischen Kirche assoziiert wird. Allerdings wäre die Behauptung irreführend, Büttners Werk habe ein Sujet und kreise um ein mit dieser Religion oder zum Beispiel der Armut verbundenes Thema oder Denken. Tatsächlich handelt ihr Werk nicht „von" etwas. Es stellt keine Bezüge zu einer Tradition oder zu bestimmten moralischen und ästhetischen Werten her, sondern „entwickelt" sich daraus. Es ist schwer, einen bestimmten Holzschnitt, eine Glasmalerei oder ein Video herauszulösen und zu verstehen, was dahinter steht. Gleichzeitig wäre es auch falsch zu behaupten, eine Gruppe ihrer Arbeiten bilde eine „Installation". Büttners Werke reagieren nicht an erster Stelle auf den sie umgebenden Raum, auch wenn sie sich offensichtlich zu ihm verhalten. Man kann sich leicht auf ein bestimmtes Stück konzentrieren, aber Sinn machen die einzelnen Werke nur, wenn man sie zueinander in Beziehung setzt. Jedes Teil besitzt eine dialogische Beziehung zur Gesamtheit ihrer künstlerischen Praxis. Anders ausgedrückt: Die einzelnen Werke dienen nicht dazu, ein Thema zu illustrieren, sondern wollen auf das Problem hinweisen, das sich durch das gesamte Œuvre von Andrea Büttner zieht. Wie können wir über ein neues Leben nachdenken?

Insofar as people are born, they are new beginnings

Life blows open that what cannot be absorbed by concepts. Life itself is proof of the fact that new beginnings are possible. And, insofar as they are new beginnings, new beginnings can be instigated.

The nature of the myth of a new beginning, its ethical and aesthetic implications for life as well as art, is at the core of Andrea Büttner's interest in poverty, love and certain aspects of the Catholic doctrine. The tension between the realm of the ideal and the immediate here and now, as well as the fact that a human's act can change not only their own life, but life understood in a broader sense, are questions present in her work through two notions that are intimately related: faith and hope. Change depends on hope, and hope is another name for a new life, a different start, a new beginning.

The question of the political is always tied to the notion of freedom and action. If people are free, they are free to act. Hope relates directly to the possibility to act, of being able to illuminate life with a sense of the possible, and the avoidance of evil. The connection Andrea Büttner's work has with certain forms of the Catholic faith derives from one pivotal question: the function of nativity. People are new beginnings who also embody the capacity of producing new beginnings. In this light, freedom is not a disposition that eventually allows people to become self-sufficient and autonomous, but is a fundamental characteristic that we all carry from birth. Freedom is the possibility of the unprecedented, like a new life.

In omnibus caritas

The notion of *caritas* – of care, neighbourly love – stands in radical opposition to the idea of the self-contained, and therefore is also

Der Mensch wird geboren. Insofern ist er ein Neuanfang

Was Konzepte nicht absorbieren können, wird vom Leben gesprengt. Der Beweis für die Möglichkeit des Neuanfangs ist das Leben selbst. Und wenn es den Neuanfang gibt, kann er auch initiiert werden.

Der Mythos des Neuanfangs, seine ethischen und ästhetischen Implikationen, ob für das Leben oder die Kunst, steht im Zentrum von Andrea Büttners Interesse an Armut, Liebe und bestimmten Aspekten der katholischen Lehre. Zwei verwandte Begriffe kennzeichnen die Spannung zwischen dem Reich des Idealen und dem unmittelbaren Hier und Jetzt in ihrem Werk, aber auch die Tatsache, dass das Handeln eines Menschen nicht nur sein eigenes, sondern auch das Leben in einem allgemeineren Sinne verändern kann: Glauben und Hoffnung. Veränderung braucht Hoffnung, und Hoffnung ist ein anderer Name für ein neues Leben, für einen anderen, neuen Anfang.

Das Politische ist immer an die Begriffe von Freiheit und Handeln gebunden. Wenn Menschen frei sind, dann sind sie frei zu handeln. Hoffnung ist unmittelbar auf die Möglichkeit des Handelns bezogen, auf die Fähigkeit, das Leben mit einem Gefühl des Möglichen zu erhellen und das Böse zu vermeiden. Die Beziehungen zu bestimmten Formen des katholischen Glaubens in Andrea Büttners Werk entstehen aus der entscheidenden Frage nach der Funktion der Geburt. Der Mensch ist ein Neuanfang, der auch die Fähigkeit verkörpert, neue Anfänge herzustellen. So gesehen ist Freiheit keine Neigung, die Menschen allmählich autark und autonom werden lässt, sondern ein grundlegendes Merkmal, das wir alle von Geburt an in uns tragen. Freiheit ist die Möglichkeit des Noch-nie-da-gewesenen, wie ein neues Leben.

We are people of the spectacle.

related to another important subject in the work of Andrea Büttner: shame. *Caritas* encompasses one of the most complex systems in which to place human relations. It is different from friendship and love, and, unlike the other two terms, it has controversial political implications. In her dissertation on Saint Augustine, the political philosopher Hannah Arendt argues that Christian *caritas* is worldless, and therefore anti-political.[1] It would be difficult in a text about art to discuss the philosophical arguments that bring both Saint Augustine and Arendt to analyse the question of *caritas*, were it not for the fact that the fundamental role *caritas* and poverty play in the early development of Christianity is key to Büttner's interest in this religion.

If *caritas* is an action that develops independently of its context and of the world in which it takes place, one could agree with Arendt that it is indeed anti-political. However, if it is a response or reaction to certain states or conditions, it becomes a political action: it becomes charity. Büttner's study of several orders of nuns can be seen in the light of this radical paradox. The paradox between those who act because they promised to act *in caritas*, and those who believe their actions respond to the possibility of making a difference, of transforming the world. The artist's work emerges from this fruitful tension: between a modern and pre-modern understanding of freedom, of our acting-in-the world. The modern mind understands charity, or aid, as a way to rehabilitate a temporary loss of autonomy of the subject. The pre-modern, or, to be more specific, the Augustinean understanding of 'I' relates to a vote, and to a permanent engagement with the fact that self-sufficiency is impossible on earth.

In omnibus caritas

Der Begriff der Caritas – Fürsorge, Nächstenliebe – steht in radikalem Gegensatz zum Begriff der Unabhängigkeit und ist deshalb auch mit einem anderen wichtigen Thema in Büttners Werk verwandt: der Scham. Unter Caritas versteht man eines der komplexesten Systeme menschlicher Beziehungen. Sie unterscheidet sich von Freundschaft und Liebe und anders als bei diesen sind ihre politischen Implikationen umstritten. Die politische Philosophin Hannah Arendt bezeichnet die christliche Caritas in ihrer Dissertation über Augustinus als weltlos und deshalb antipolitisch.[1] Es ist sicher problematisch, in einem Text über Kunst die philosophischen Argumente für die Analyse der Caritas bei Augustinus und Arendt zu diskutieren, wäre da nicht die Tatsache, dass der Schlüssel zu Büttners Interesse an dieser Religion in eben der fundamentalen Bedeutung von Caritas und Armut in der frühen Entwicklung des Christentums liegt.

Ist Caritas unabhängig von dem Kontext und der Welt, in der sie handelt, dann ließe sich mit Arendt feststellen, dass sie antipolitisch ist. Ist sie aber eine Antwort oder Reaktion auf bestimmte Zustände oder Bedingungen, wird sie zur politischen Handlung: zur Wohltätigkeit. Man kann Büttners Studien über verschiedene Nonnenorden vor dem Hintergrund dieses radikalen Gegensatzes sehen: dem Gegensatz zwischen einem Handeln „in caritas", das einem Gelübde entspringt, und einem Handeln im Glauben an die Möglichkeit, die Welt zu verändern. Das Kunstwerk entsteht aus dieser fruchtbaren Spannung zwischen einem modernen und einem vormodernen Verständnis von Freiheit und unserem Handeln in der Welt. Nach modernem Verständnis ist Wohltätigkeit oder Hilfe ein Weg, den zeitweisen Autonomieverlust dessen, der Hilfe benötigt, zu beheben. Das vormoderne, oder genauer, das augustinische

If you wear red it tires you
out after a while, no?

When everyone, artists, they feel that
certain colours go well together...

Disparates

Büttner's choice of the woodcut as a technique to work with
responds to an interest in notions originating before the modern
period, related to life, freedom, change, poverty, precariousness
and the relationships one can, must, or may establish with
others. As with every medium, the woodcut comes with a formal,
aesthetic and political language. The technique dates back to
fourth-century Japan, and was subsequently used in China. The
first-known woodcuts in Europe date back to the eighth century,
although it was only from the fourteenth century onwards that
this printing technique became more widely used for the reproduction of religious images, such as ex-votos placed at altarpieces
or attached to clothes to protect people from evil. The woodcut
never enjoyed a fully modern life, as other engraving and printing
techniques had a more prominent position. Due to its nature,
a woodcut has a very specific directness, a simplicity of line,
an economy of means and a relationship with colour that very
strongly determines its syntax. The nature and roots of this visual
language are very present in the work of Andrea Büttner. It is not
that she wants to 'win' an ancient technique for 'our times', on
the contrary, she wants us to get absorbed by the oceanic quality
of its motifs. The flatness of their colours bears the quality of the
unlimited, like the ocean. The figures on them are grounded
by this colour place, which holds them in an immobile equilibrium,
making it possible for form to be seen, to appear.
This condition of colour holding form occurs in her work to such
an extent that the element encompassed – the figure – assumes
a secondary role, that of casting into the loathsome depth anything
that may have remained. Like the Ocean for Gilles Deleuze, the
colour here marks the realm of the unbound, unconstrained and

Verständnis des „Ich" bezieht sich auf eine Wahlmöglichkeit
und auf eine permanente Auseinandersetzung mit der Unmöglich-
keit der Autonomie auf Erden.

Disparitäten

Büttners Entscheidung für die Technik des Holzschnitts entspringt
ihrem Interesse an einem ursprünglich vormodernen Begriff
von Leben, Freiheit, Veränderung, Armut, Unsicherheit und den
Beziehungen, die man zu anderen herstellen kann und muss.
Wie jedes Medium hat auch der Holzschnitt seine eigene formale,
ästhetische und politische Sprache. Die Technik geht auf das
4. Jahrhundert in Japan zurück und fand anschließend ihren Weg
nach China. Die ersten bekannten Holzschnitte in Europa datieren
aus dem 8. Jahrhundert, auch wenn religiöse Bilder erst seit dem
14. Jahrhundert dank der Drucktechnik in größerem Umfang
reproduziert wurden, etwa als Votivbilder, die an Altären oder zum
Schutz vor dem Bösen an der Kleidung angebracht wurden. Der
Holzschnitt stand in der Moderne immer im Schatten anderer
Gravur- und Drucktechniken. Seine Syntax wird durch die ihm
eigenen Merkmale geprägt – die spezifische Unmittelbarkeit, die
Einfachheit der Linienführung, die Ökonomie der Mittel und
die Beziehung zur Farbe. Wesen und Wurzeln dieser Bildsprache
sind in Andrea Büttners Werk sehr präsent. Es geht ihr nicht
darum, eine alte Technik „für unsere Zeit zurückzuerobern",
vielmehr sollen wir uns von der ozeanischen Qualität seiner Motive
absorbieren lassen. Die Flächigkeit der Farben vermittelt eine
Qualität des Unbegrenzten, nicht anders als der Ozean. Die Figuren
werden durch diese Farben geerdet, so dass sie bewegungslos
im Gleichgewicht bleiben und es der Form ermöglichen, gesehen
zu werden, zu erscheinen.

free. There is no surprise, then, that in many of Büttner's works colour appears on its own. These monochrome pieces do not only stress this reverse relationship between background and figure, but, more importantly, they re-state the importance of the dimension of time in the work. When colour re-appears, alone, without a figure, it introduces a sense of return, of repetition. A repetition that addresses another repetition: the fact that the chosen colours are indeed 'repeating' existing colours, existing codes. A blue could have been taken from the cloth of a religious order, or a religious scene in a fresco, for example. Colour does repeat, and, at the same time, it does not. The blue, the brown, the pale pink or the red that Büttner uses are radically different on a piece of paper, or used on the wall, than they were in the cloth used by certain nuns, or in a fresco on the wall of a church. The monochromes make it obvious that a repetition, of a colour, of a thing, is never a real repetition. But it is also important to understand that the aim of repetition is not resemblance: it is not meant to be identified with a subject. That is, the repeated blue Büttner uses on paper does not seek to be identical or identified with the blue worn by nuns, for example. These colours, that resemble other colours that also exist in the outside world, are used as symbols and as representations, not bridges. They do not try to carry us to a past time, to locate a point of connection with a world of virtues and an aesthetic of living that belongs to religion. No. These colours actually affirm that the difference is there, present, unavoidable. Using Deleuze's words, the colours, and by extension the other motifs constantly appearing in her woodcuts, such as the books, the tents, the stones, the birds..., are disparates. Disparity is a quality something acquires when, after being repeated, something else, dissimilar to the 'original' appears.

Dieser Zustand der von der Farbe gehaltenen Form ist in Büttners Werk so eindringlich, dass das festgehaltene Element – die Figur – eine sekundäre Rolle spielt: Ihre Aufgabe ist es, das, was geblieben sein mag, in die finsteren Tiefen zu werfen. Wie der Ozean für Gilles Deleuze, so markiert hier die Farbe den Bereich des Ungebundenen, der Ungezwungenheit und Freiheit. Deshalb verwundert es nicht, dass die Farbe bei Büttner so oft für sich allein steht. Diese Einfarbigkeit betont allerdings nicht nur die Umkehrbeziehung von Hintergrund und Figur, sondern formuliert vor allem auch eine neue Bedeutung der Dimension von Zeit im Werk. Die Farbe, die ohne eine Figur allein wiedererscheint, löst ein Gefühl der Wiederkehr, der Wiederholung aus. Eine Wiederholung, die auf eine andere verweist: Die gewählten Farben „wiederholen" real existierende Farben, existierende Codes. Ein Blau kann zum Beispiel von der Kleidung eines religiösen Ordens oder von einer religiösen Szene in einem Fresko stammen. Die Farbe wiederholt und wiederholt zugleich auch nicht. Das Blau, Braun, Hellrosa oder Rot, das Büttner benutzt, ist auf dem Blatt Papier oder der Wand radikal anders als in dem Stoff eines Nonnenhabits oder im Fresko auf einer Kirchenwand. Durch die Einfarbigkeit wird offensichtlich, dass eine Wiederholung, sei es bei einer Farbe oder einer Sache, nie eine wirkliche Wiederholung ist. Wichtig ist aber auch, dass die Wiederholung nicht auf Ähnlichkeit zielt: sie soll nicht mit einem Sujet identifiziert werden. Das heißt, die Wiederholung des Blaus auf dem Papier ist weder identisch mit dem Blau, das zum Beispiel Nonnen tragen, noch sollte es damit identifiziert werden. Diese Farben, die anderen, auch in der Welt vorhandenen Farben ähneln, Symbole und Repräsentationen, sind keine Brücken. Sie sollen uns nicht in eine vergangene Zeit versetzen, keinen Ort lokalisieren, an dem sich eine einer Religion zugehörige Welt der Tugend mit

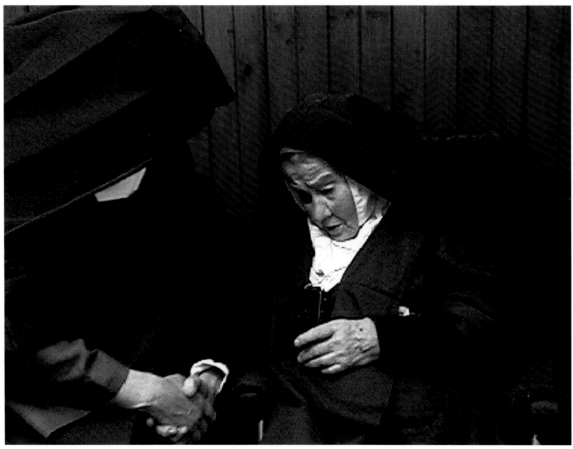

So, one could say that a disparate is already a new beginning. The possibility of something different appearing establishes an idea of time that is not identical with linear time. These works, the motifs, the colours, the references present in them are not happening as an aftermath, they do not constitute a 'new' interpretation of the world that is alive in them. They are radically different from the world of religion, from the beliefs, from the virtues, from the aesthetics at play, from the individuals that live the doctrine. The work is a disparate appearing from all of it. A totally different real than the real that is present in the life of the people Büttner's videos portray, or in the found little objects she adds sometimes to the display of her works, or in the pictures of herself, or the images of her parents visiting a church, or the Xeroxed copies of motifs that interest her... All her works share a balance, a sense of peace. However, there is tension in the rooms in which the work appears. A tension produced by the correspondence between two worlds, the world of individuals and their institutions and the world of art, representation, aesthetics. A tension caused as well by the juxtaposition of two types of judgement: moral judgement, present in life seen through people, and aesthetic judgement, a fundamental part of our understanding of a work and its relevance.

This tension addresses the currently most uncomfortable subject, one that all 'politically conscious' art tries to negate: the separation between art and knowledge. The separation of knowledge from art is irreversible. There is no such a thing as 'the production of knowledge' by art, or, at least, not in these terms. A consciousness, or, to be more precise, an artistic consciousness in which perception and concept, image and sign would be one, is not, if it ever existed, to be re-created. Its restitution would be a return to chaos.

---

einer Ästhetik des Lebens verbindet. Nein, diese Farben bestätigen den vorhandenen und unvermeidlichen Unterschied. Sie und damit auch die anderen Motive, die ständig in Büttners Holzschnitten auftauchen, etwa Bücher, Zelte, Steine, Vögel usw., sind Disparitäten im Sinne von Deleuze. Disparität ist eine Eigenschaft, die dann etwas annehmen kann, wenn nach der Wiederholung etwas anderes auftaucht, das dem „Original" unähnlich ist.

Man könnte also sagen, dass Disparität schon ein Neuanfang ist. Die Möglichkeit, dass etwas anderes erscheint, begründet eine Vorstellung von Zeit, die nicht identisch ist mit der linearen Zeit. Diese Arbeiten mit ihren Motiven, Farben und Bezügen sind kein Nachspiel, sie interpretieren die Welt, die in ihnen lebt, nicht „neu".

Sie unterscheiden sich radikal von der Welt der Religion, vom Glauben, von den Tugenden, von der Ästhetik, die dabei im Spiel ist, und von den Individuen, die die Lehre leben. Das Werk ist eine Disparität, die aus all dem auftaucht. Es ist eine völlig andere Realität als die Realität der Menschen, die Büttners Videos portraitieren, der kleinen „Objets trouvés", die sie ihren Arbeiten bei Ausstellungen manchmal mitgibt, der Selbstbildnisse, der Bilder ihrer Eltern in einer Kirche oder der Kopien von Motiven, die sie interessieren...All ihren Werken ist ein Gleichgewicht gemeinsam, ein Gefühl der Ruhe. In den Räumen allerdings, in denen die Werke zu sehen sind, gibt es Spannung. Eine durch die Korrespondenz zweier Welten – der Welt der Individuen mit ihren Institutionen und der Welt der Kunst, der Repräsentation, der Ästhetik – produzierte Spannung, die ihre Ursache auch in der Gegenüberstellung von zwei Varianten des Urteils hat: dem moralischen Urteil, das im Leben durch den Blick des Menschen präsent ist, und dem ästhetischen Urteil, das grundlegend zu unserem Verständnis eines Werks und seiner Bedeutung gehört.

The detritus of a hermeneutic psychology has to appear under a strange new form of political expressionism, simply because the political thought can entrust itself to the violence that image and concept bestow upon one another. Instead, a jargon of authenticity in which words tremble and images seem paralysed has possessed a region of the 'good' art world, allowing moral judgement to be the one ruling among cultural categories used again by modern-day philistines.

The work of Andrea Büttner is very ambitious in that it is an almost silent denunciation of poetic montage. The work does not obey the rules of the organized art and theory game. The delusion that the order of the *ordo idearum* (to borrow Spinoza's term), the order of ideas should be the *ordo rerum*: the order of things is based on the insinuation that the mediated is unmediated. Büttner's work radically mediates; not by merging ideas into images or vice versa, but by taking an anti-systematic impulse as its own procedure and introducing concepts directly, without defining them constantly with the work, with the image. She takes the concepts as she receives them and they gain their precision only through their relation to one another. Concepts, therefore, get support from the concepts themselves, and images, similarly, get support from images. And, in doing so, the work gently defies the Cartesian – and today's neo-Cartesian – ideals of *clara et distincta perceptio* and of absolute certainty.

1

Hannah Ahrendt, *Der Liebesbegriff bei Augustin. Versuch einer philosophischen Interpretation*, published in 1929.

Diese Spannung verweist auf das heute unbehaglichste Thema, das „politische" Kunst in all ihren Formen zu negieren versucht: die Trennung zwischen Kunst und Wissen. Die Trennung des Wissens von der Kunst lässt sich nicht umkehren. Es gibt keine „Wissensproduktion durch Kunst", jedenfalls nicht in diesen Begriffen. Man kann ein Bewusstsein, oder genauer, ein künstlerisches Bewusstsein, in dem Wahrnehmung und Konzept, Bild und Zeichen eins wären, nicht erneut schaffen, falls es denn je existiert haben sollte. Seine Wiederkehr wäre die Rückkehr des Chaos. Die Reste einer hermeneutischen Psychologie müssen auf eine seltsame Art von politischem Ausdruck aufscheinen, einfach deshalb, weil das politische Denken auf die Gewalt vertrauen kann, die sich Bild und Konzept gegenseitig antun. Stattdessen aber hat ein Jargon der Eigentlichkeit, in dem die Wörter zittern und die Bilder erstarrt scheinen, von einem Bereich der „guten" Kunstwelt Besitz ergriffen und zugelassen, dass das moralische Urteil zur einzigen Ideologie unter den von heutigen Philistern wieder benutzten kulturellen Kategorien geworden ist.

Das Werk von Andrea Büttner ist insofern sehr anspruchsvoll, als es die poetische Montage fast stillschweigend denunziert. Es hält sich nicht an die Spielregeln der organisierten Kunst und Theorie. Die Verwechslung des „ordo idearum" (um Spinozas Begriff zu verwenden), also der Ordnung der Ideen, mit dem „ordo rerum", der Ordnung der Dinge, beruht auf der Unterstellung, das Vermittelte sei unvermittelt. Büttners Werk vermittelt radikal. Aber es tut dies nicht, indem es Ideen mit Bildern mischt oder umgekehrt, sondern indem es einen anti-systematischen Impuls zur Methode erhebt und Konzepte unvermittelt einführt, ohne sie ständig durch das Werk, das Bild, zu definieren. Sie nimmt die Konzepte, wie sie ihr einfallen; ihre Schärfe gewinnen sie ausschließlich durch die

Beziehungen untereinander. Deshalb werden die Konzepte von den
Konzepten und entsprechend die Bilder von den Bildern selbst
gestützt. Damit widersetzt sich ihr Werk behutsam den cartesiani-
schen – und den heutigen neo-cartesianischen – Idealen der „clara
et distincta perceptio" und der absoluten Gewissheit.

1
Hannah Arendt (1929), *Der Liebesbegriff*
bei Augustin. Versuch einer philosophischen
Interpretation, Berlin 2003.

Installation view: *Documenta 13, Neue Galerie, Kassel, Germany, 2012*

*The Archive of the Lives of the Little Sisters of Jesus with Circuses
and Fun Fairs, Tre Fontane, Rome, 2012*, slide show

The Archive of the Lives of the Little Sisters of Jesus with Circuses
and Fun Fairs, Tre Fontane, Rome, 2012

Monobloc chairs, 2010–2012, photographs, dimensions variable

Nun drawings, 2006–2007, pencil on paper sketchbook,
42 × 29.7 cm, each page

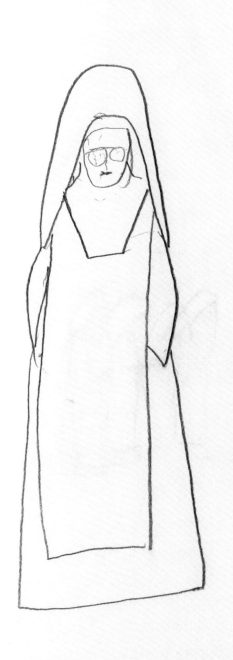

Trinkende Tiere (drinking animals), 2007, pencil and ink on paper,
29.7 × 21 cm, each sheet, drawings by Friedbert Büttner

Trinkende Tiere (drinking animals), 2007

INTERVIEW WITH ANDREA BÜTTNER
by Nikolaus Hirsch and Hans Ulrich Obrist

Hans Ulrich Obrist: Let's start at the very beginning – how did you come to art, or how did art come to you?

Andrea Büttner: Art wasn't there at the beginning. First of all I studied philosophy and – I think it may have something to do with sitting – I didn't like sitting in libraries. I wanted to do some kind of work that was more physical, and I thought about becoming either a farmer or an artist.

Nikolaus Hirsch: Your work often deals with quite everyday things. There's a piece of yours called *Little Works*. Could it be the case that – also, perhaps, because you said that you thought about becoming a farmer – a certain sense of being grounded is important to you? Is being close to little works and things essential to your investigations into the everyday?

AB: Well, the everyday is certainly important. And that's also because I'm interested in notions of a good life, or in questions that present themselves in my life. 'Little works' is a theological concept I've borrowed from others. For me, it's about exploring the poetics of 'letting fall' (*Fallen lassen*) or addressing issues such as: how much do you want to show off? To what extent can you really stand by what you do? And is it also okay to show things that you can't stand by yet? These are areas related to the concept of 'little things' or 'little works'.

HUO: *Little Works* is also an actual film, of course. There's a text by Dan Fox that includes the following description of your video piece *Little Works*: 'For which the artist gave a group of Carmelite nuns in a closed convent in West London a video camera, in order for them to document their life, in particular the creation of "little works"

INTERVIEW MIT ANDREA BÜTTNER
von Nikolaus Hirsch und Hans Ulrich Obrist

HANS ULRICH OBRIST: Um mit dem Anfang anzufangen: Wie hat alles begonnen, wie kamst du zur Kunst oder wie kam die Kunst zu dir?

ANDREA BÜTTNER: Die Kunst ist noch nicht da. Ich habe zuerst Philosophie studiert und – ich glaube, das hat mit dem Sitzen zu tun – saß nicht gern in Bibliotheken und wollte irgendeine Arbeit machen, die mehr mit dem Körper zu tun hat. Und ich hatte mir überlegt, entweder Landwirtin oder Künstlerin zu werden.

NIKOLAUS HIRSCH: Häufig geht es in deiner Arbeit um ganz alltägliche Dinge. Es gibt eine Arbeit, die heißt *Little Works*. Kann es sein, dass dir – vielleicht auch weil du gesagt hast, dass du Landwirtin werden wolltest – eine gewisse Bodenhaftung wichtig ist? Ist die Nähe zu kleinen Arbeiten und Dingen eine Voraussetzung für dich, um dich mit Alltäglichem zu beschäftigen?

AB: Also es ist schon wichtig, das Alltägliche. Und zwar auch, weil es mir um gutes Leben geht oder um Fragen, die ich durch mein Leben habe. *Little Works* – das ist ein theologischer Begriff, den habe ich ja von anderen übernommen. Mir geht es da um eine Poetik des Fallenlassens oder um solche Fragen: Wie angeberisch will man eigentlich sein? Oder wie sehr kann man eigentlich zu dem stehen, was man macht? Und ist es auch okay, Dinge zu zeigen, zu denen man noch gar nicht stehen kann? Das sind Bereiche, die mit dem Begriff der „kleinen Dinge" oder der „kleinen Arbeiten" zu tun haben.

HUO: *Little Works* ist ja auch ein konkreter Film. Es gibt einen Text von Dan Fox, in dem er das Video *Little Works* beschreibt: „For which the artist gave a group of Carmelite nunsin a closed convent

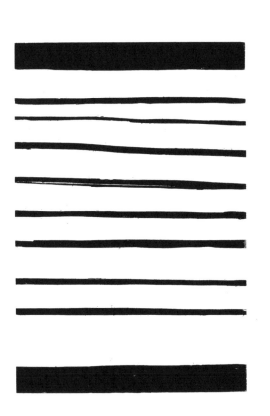

– small votive offerings made by each nun in the form of craft works (...)"[1] Could you maybe tell us something about that?

AB: I moved to a new place in London and saw on the map that there was a Carmelite convent nearby. Then I happened to see a nun on the bus and she got off at the same stop as me, so I plucked up my courage and spoke to her. That was the start of my relationship, or friendship, with this group of nuns. It's a subject that interests me generally – nuns who make art, that parallel world of art that exists within the church. Of course it's just one of the many parallel art worlds that exist. Anyway, these Carmelite nuns make objects, crocheted baskets and painted icons, which they refer to as 'little works'. Once a year, they display the things they've produced over the past year and give them as gifts to other members of the group. My video is in fact a piece about their art.

HUO: There appears to be an underlying principle, which, although it doesn't apply to all of your work, does crop up frequently: the idea of collaborating as opposed to working on your own. It seems that your art often involves some form of collaboration and that other people also contribute to your work. For example, there are the drawings your father was involved in making.

AB: It's true – I often work with other people on things. And the reasons for this vary greatly from one work to the next. In my father's case, for example, it was because he does actually send me drawings, and also the fact that he can draw very well, but is not an artist himself. That's something I'd like to show. So it's a question of what can actually be shown in an exhibition space, or what really belongs in the realm of art? And often I don't have any ideas of my own and so I ask other people for theirs – as Andy Warhol did too.

NH: That goes back to what you were talking about earlier: the problematic issue of showing. At the Royal College of Art in

in West London a video camera in order for them to document their life, in particular the creation of 'little works' - small votive offerings made by each nun in theform of craft works (...)"[1] Kannst du dazu etwas sagen?

AB: Ich bin in London umgezogen und habe auf dem Stadtplan gesehen, dass ein Karmelitinnen-Kloster ganz in der Nähe ist. Durch Zufall habe ich dann im Bus eine Nonne getroffen und sie ist an der gleichen Haltestelle ausgestiegen wie ich. Ich habe mir ein Herz gefasst und sie angesprochen. Und ich habe eine Beziehung oder eine Freundschaft mit dieser Gruppe von Nonnen angefangen. Also ich interessiere mich überhaupt für Nonnen, die Kunst machen; für diese parallele Kunstwelt, die es in der Kirche gibt. Das ist natürlich nur eine der vielen parallelen Kunstwelten, die es gibt. Und diese Karmelitinnen machen eben Objekte, häkeln Körbchen und malen Ikonen. Sie nennen das *Little Works*. Die Dinge, die sie übers Jahr hin machen, stellen sie einmal pro Jahr aus und verschenken sie innerhalb der Gruppe. Mein Video ist eigentlich eine Arbeit über ihre Kunst.

HUO: Es scheint ein Prinzip zu geben, das in deiner Arbeit nicht immer, aber oft, auftaucht: Die Idee einer Zusammenarbeit im Unterschied zum Alleine-Arbeiten. Es scheint bei dir oft so zu sein, dass es zu einer Zusammenarbeit kommt und dass auch andere Teilnehmer oder Teilnehmerinnen etwas für dein Werk tun. Es gibt zum Beispiel diese Zeichnungen von dir, an denen dein Vater beteiligt war.

AB: Das stimmt, es kommt oft vor, dass ich mit anderen etwas mache. Und zwar aus unterschiedlichsten Gründen in den unterschiedlichen Arbeiten. Bei meinem Vater zum Beispiel, weil er wirklich Zeichnungen an mich schickt, und weil es mir auch darum ging, dass er gut zeichnen kann, aber selbst kein Künstler ist. Das

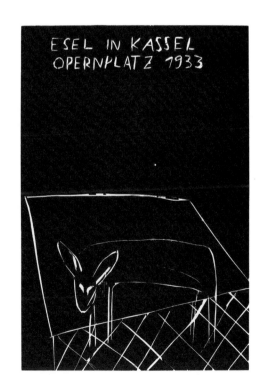

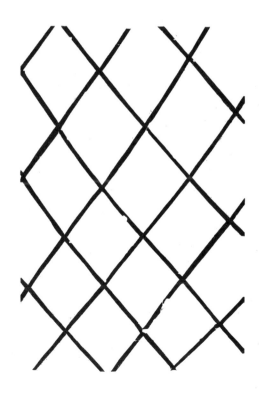

London you wrote your PhD thesis on 'Shame and Art'. Can you tell us something about the difficulty of this act of showing, and about the shame involved in the practice of making art?

AB: Well, there's a well-established discourse on contemporary visual culture which argues that it's a culture of shamelessness. Twitter and YouTube, for example, are part of this discourse. However, I noticed that I don't actually feel all that free, or that I feel ashamed about many things. And that has nothing at all to do with what you show. I simply took this feeling seriously and have now spent a long time thinking about it. I think there's a structural connection between doing something in the seclusion of the studio and the act of showing, exhibiting and thereby exposing it to the judgement of others. This also reflects how we perceive and value art in our culture – Kant, of course, wrote on the subject of aesthetic judgement. According to what criteria do we consider something to be good? Norms are inscribed in this evaluation process, as are the criteria for high or low, large or small. And these are the issues I am addressing.

HUO: At the Hollybush Gardens gallery in London you recently presented the exhibition *HAP Grieshaber – Der Engel der Geschichte (The Angel of History)*. This, too, was about a protest against forgetting, in the form of a magazine by the artist HAP Grieshaber that has fallen into oblivion. Grieshaber published 25 issues of *Engel der Geschichte*, which follows on from Walter Benjamin. What prompted you to focus on Grieshaber and his magazine?

AB: I was particularly interested in this magazine because it was a collaborative project and Grieshaber often invited his friends to write something for it or to contribute graphic works. The magazines always addressed political themes – taking a stance against whaling, for example, or against the dictatorship in Greece. In

möchte ich zeigen. Also was kann man eigentlich im Ausstellungsraum zeigen oder was gehört zum Bereich der Kunst? Oft habe ich auch keine Ideen und frage andere, das hat ja auch Andy Warhol gemacht.

NH: Das ist wieder diese Schwierigkeit, von der du anfangs sprachst: Das Problem des Zeigens. Du hast am Royal College of Art in London deinen PhD zu „Shame and Art" gemacht. Kannst du etwas zur Schwierigkeit dieses Zeigens und der Scham bei der Praxis des Kunstmachens sagen?

AB: Also es gibt einen bekannten Diskurs über die zeitgenössische visuelle Kultur, dass sie eine Kultur der Schamlosigkeit sei. Twitter und YouTube – das gehört zum Beispiel zu diesem Diskurs. Ich habe aber gemerkt, dass ich mich eigentlich gar nicht so frei fühle oder mich für viele Dinge schäme. Und das hat gar nichts damit zu tun, was man zeigt. Ich habe einfach dieses Gefühl ernst genommen und denke jetzt schon lange darüber nach. Ich denke, es gibt einen strukturellen Zusammenhang zwischen etwas im Atelier im Verborgenen tun und es zeigen, ausstellen und es damit dem Urteil anderer aussetzen. Das liegt auch daran, wie man in unserer Kultur mit Kunst umgeht – über das ästhetische Urteil hat ja Kant geschrieben. Nach welchen Kriterien findet man Dinge gut: Da schreiben sich Normen ein oder Kriterien für Hohes oder Niedriges, für Großes oder Kleines. Ja, um diese Themen geht es mir.

HUO: Vor kurzem hast du in der Londoner Galerie Hollybush Gardens die Ausstellung *HAP Grieshaber – Der Engel der Geschichte* gezeigt. Da geht es auch wieder um Protest gegen das Vergessen, um eine Zeitschrift von HAP Grieshaber, die ins Vergessen geraten ist. Er hat 25 Nummern der Zeitschrift „Engel der Geschichte" veröffentlicht, was ja auch an Walter Benjamin anschließt und an

recent years there have been debates within visual art about the political dimension of the judgement of taste per se. I found it interesting to revisit political discourses in art that are very traditionally thematic and based on committed engagement. Another aspect is of course the fact that I make woodcuts. Grieshaber was responsible for the development of the post-expressionist woodcut in the 1950s. And there's also a biographical connection: in return for allowing him to depict them in his work *Osterritt*, Grieshaber taught a group of Franciscan nuns how to do woodcuts, and one of these women who had learnt woodcutting from him was later my teacher at school. A huge woodcut by Grieshaber also hung in the secretary's office there, and that was the first artwork I encountered as a child.

HUO: I'd like to know more about the woodcuts. On the subject of artistic skills you once said: 'One aspect of the woodcuts is certainly skill, or the fact that it is important that there is one area in my work where I produce something beautiful (...).'[2] While you have these quite diverse collaborative projects, most of the woodcuts are not the result of cooperation. So what role do the woodcuts play? What's the common thread running through your work as a whole?

AB: I started making woodcuts in the 1990s, and that no doubt had something to do with the fact that woodcutting was really an 1980s medium, and was associated with things like gesturalism à la Baselitz, the cult of genius, or all these other discourses that were taboo in the 1990s. For me, making woodcuts had on the one hand always been a very familiar practice, and then it was certainly motivated by the desire to do something uncool. But that's not important to me now as a reason for doing it. It's simply that I like having one area where I can be physically engaged using an angle

---

das, was Axel Honneth ganz am Anfang des Marathons über Benjamin sagte. Was hat dich veranlasst, dich mit Grieshaber und seiner Zeitschrift zu beschäftigen?

AB: Ich habe mich speziell mit dieser Zeitschrift beschäftigt, weil sie ein kollaboratives Projekt ist und Grieshaber häufig seine Freundinnen und Freunde eingeladen hat, darin zu schreiben oder Graphiken beizusteuern. Es geht in dieser Zeitschrift immer um politische Themen: Gegen Walfang oder gegen die Diktatur in Griechenland. Es gab in den letzten Jahren Diskurse in der bildenden Kunst über das Politische des Geschmacksurteils als solches. Ich fand es interessant, zurückzugehen zu politischen Diskursen in der Kunst, die ganz klassisch thematisch sind und die mit Engagement zu tun haben. Eine andere Sache ist natürlich, dass ich Holzschnitte mache. Grieshaber ist derjenige, der den nachexpressionistischen Holzschnitt in die Fünfzigerjahre übersetzt hat. Und es gibt noch einen biographischen Zusammenhang: Er hat einer Gruppe von franziskanischen Nonnen das Holzschnitt-Machen beigebracht im Gegenzug dafür, dass er sie im *Osterritt* abgebildet hat. Eine dieser Frauen, die von ihm den Holzschnitt gelernt hat, war dann meine Lehrerin in der Schule. Dort hing ein Riesenholzschnitt von Grieshaber im Sekretariat. Das war das erste Kunstwerk, das ich als Kind kennen gelernt habe.

HUO: Ich würde gerne mehr über die Holzschnitte wissen. Es gibt einen Satz von dir, indem es um Skills geht: „One aspect of the woodcuts is certainly skill, or the fact that it is important that there is one area in my work where I produce something beautiful (...)."[2] Während es diese ganz verschiedenen kollaborativen Projekte gibt, sind die meisten Holzschnitte ja nicht durch eine Zusammenarbeit entstanden. Was ist die Rolle der Holzschnitte? Was ist der rote Faden, der sich durch das ganze Werk zieht?

grinder. And besides that, it's important to have something that is connected to reproduction techniques and Pop Art, but still has its own aura somehow.

HUO: Farming is the big unrealized project. Do you have any other unrealized projects?

AB: Yes, I'm very interested in mosses at the moment. It's really Duchamp's dust, but in nature I see moss everywhere.

HUO: Is that a research project?

AB: No, not really. I'd simply like to do something with moss – I'm not sure what, exactly – and now I see that mosses are everywhere. Yes, and I'd also like to do a book – a picture book on 'Critiqueof Judgement'.

NH: The ambivalent yet productive relationship between theory and practice runs through your work. You did a PhD and you continue to write. Recently you wrote something for a Dieter Roth exhibition in New York. How important is writing to you?

AB: I find writing extremely difficult, and I always think I should do more of it. For example, I've been thinking about poverty a lot recently, and I think that's a subject I'd like to write more about. It's easy to write a thesis at university – then it's clear what form the text has to take. Now I am realizing that it's important to me, but I'm not sure how to go about it yet.

NH: What form did the text on Dieter Roth take?

AB: It was an academic essay. That's easy.

NH: How important is Dieter Roth to your work?

AB: Dieter Roth is very important to my work. I've thought a lot about shame, and Dieter Roth did too. There's a wonderful book published by Barbara Wien – the collected interviews of Dieter Roth – where he talks about shame all the time. It's actually very therapeutic to read this book. It revolves around the question

AB: Angefangen habe ich damit in den Neunzigern und es hatte bestimmt damit zu tun, dass Holzschnitte natürlich ein Achtzigerjahre-Medium waren und mit so was wie Baselitz-Gestischem, Geniekult oder allen möglichen Diskursen, die in den Neunzigern Tabu waren, verbunden war. Der Holzschnitt war mir schon immer so nah, und es war sicher das Bedürfnis, etwas Uncooles zu machen. Aber das interessiert mich jetzt nicht mehr so als Grund. Ich glaube, es hat auch diese Funktion der Landwirtschaft in meinem Leben übernommen. Es ist wirklich so, dass ich es einfach mag, dass es etwas gibt, wo ich mit der Flex körperlich hantieren kann. Und dann ist es wichtig, etwas zu haben, das mit Reproduktion und mit Pop zu tun hat, aber was doch irgendwie eine ganz eigene Aura hat.

HUO: Die Landwirtschaft ist das große unrealisierte Projekt. Gibt es andere unrealisierte Projekte?

AB: Ja, Moose interessieren mich gerade. Eigentlich ist das der Staub von Duchamp, aber in der Natur, da sehe ich überall Moose.

HUO: Ist das eine Recherche?

AB: Nein, eine Recherche eher nicht. Ich möchte einfach gerne etwas mit Moosen machen was, weiß ich gar nicht, und jetzt sehe ich, dass sie überall sind. Ja, und ein Buch möchte ich gerne machen: ein Bilderbuch zur „Kritik der Urteilskraft".

NH: Das ambivalente, aber produktive Verhältnis zwischen Theorie und Praxis, zieht sich durch deine Arbeit. Du hast einen PhD gemacht und schreibst auch nach wie vor. Neulich hast du für eine Ausstellung von Dieter Roth in New York geschrieben. Wie wichtig ist das Schreiben für dich?

AB: Das Schreiben fällt mir unheimlich schwer, und ich denke immer, ich sollte es mehr machen. Zum Beispiel denke ich in letzter Zeit viel über Armut nach, und ich denke, eigentlich ist das ein

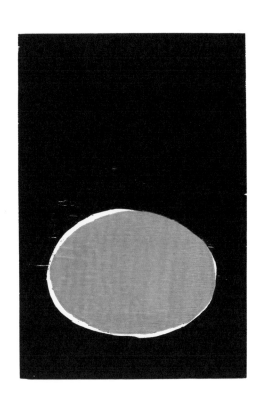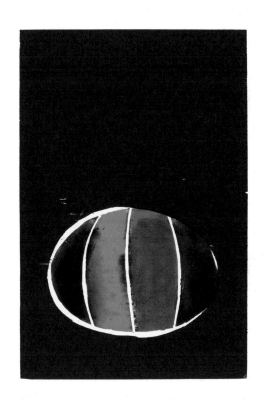

of how much you show, what you show, and how you live up to the expectations – the projected expectations – of the audience. These are questions that run through the work, and do so in a way that is not necessarily visible. And these are subjects I'm very interested in. For example, Roth's art often incorporated leftovers and rubbish and mould – which is also similar to moss. Roth worked with rubbish because he said he was ashamed of his drawings and paintings until he discovered that if he poured something over them it was a relief for him. The mould generates its own beauty. Often people think that mould is disgusting, but it's actually beautiful compared to those ugly pictures he himself created. I can completely understand that. Roth is important to me because his work has a lot to do with shame, but it's not always visible.

HUO: Roth was also a book-producing machine. There are hundreds of books by him – an incredible body of work. And there were always connections to literature, so one can say he was as much a poet as he was a writer and a visual artist, besides which he very often collaborated with other artists.

AB: And with his family.

HUO: With his family, with his son Bjorn and with lots of different people. We haven't discussed yet whether your work involves collaboration with other fields, whether you collaborate with scientists, say, or poets.

AB: I've just been collaborating with people from different fields, above all with artists, whom I asked to give me instructions on how to let something fall. I didn't just ask artists but also curators, and a writer. What was interesting was that their answers – in other words the instructions they gave me – were influenced by their respective disciplines. I've just realized that there's another form of collaboration with curators, namely in the interviews I conduct

---

Thema, über das ich mehr schreiben möchte. Es ist leicht, an der Uni eine Doktorarbeit zu schreiben. Dann ist es klar, in welche Form das kommt. Jetzt merke ich, es ist mir doch wichtig, aber ich weiß noch nicht wie.

NH: Welche Form hat der Text über Dieter Roth?

AB: Das war ein akademischer Essay. Das ist einfach.

NH: Wie wichtig ist Dieter Roth für deine Arbeit?

AB: Dieter Roth ist ganz wichtig für meine Arbeit. Ich habe viel über Scham nachgedacht und Dieter Roth auch. Es gibt ein wunderschönes Buch, das Barbara Wien herausgegeben hat: die gesammelten Interviews von Dieter Roth. Darin spricht er ununterbrochen über Scham. Eigentlich ist es sehr therapeutisch, dieses Buch zu lesen. Es geht um die Frage: Wie viel zeigt man und was zeigt man und wie wird man den Ansprüchen, den projizierten Ansprüchen des Publikums eigentlich gerecht. Das sind Fragen, die sich durch das Werk ziehen – und zwar auch in einer Weise, die man gar nicht unbedingt sieht. Das sind Themen, die mich sehr interessieren. Roth hat ja zum Beispiel viel mit Resten und Abfall und Schimmel gearbeitet – was auch ähnlich ist wie Moos. Roth hat mit Abfall gearbeitet, weil er sagte, dass er sich für die Zeichnungen und die Malereien, die er gemacht hat, geschämt hat, bis er gemerkt hat, dass es eine Erleichterung für ihn bedeutet, wenn er etwas drüberschüttet. Der Schimmel erzeugt eine eigene Schönheit. Es wird oft gedacht, Schimmel sei etwas Ekelhaftes, aber in Wirklichkeit ist es eine Schönheit im Vergleich zu diesen hässlichen Bildern, die er selbst gemacht hat. Das kann ich gut verstehen. Roth ist wichtig für mich, weil es viel um Scham geht, aber man es nicht unbedingt sieht.

HUO: Roth war auch eine Buchmaschine. Hunderte von Büchern gibt es von ihm, ein unglaubliches Werk. Es gab auch immer

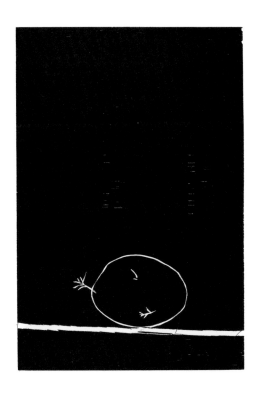
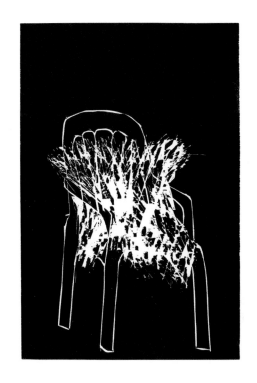

where I pose questions to critics or curators as if they were actually the artists. That's one area where I work with people from other disciplines.

HUO: So you've compiled instructions on how to let things fall. Is that going to lead to a film or a book?

AB: No, it's an exhibition. In fact, the installation of the exhibition – the set-up period – will be spent letting things fall, and the traces of this activity will then constitute the work.

HUO: One last question, perhaps, on changing one's location: I read an interview with Dieter Roth where he talks about the importance of relocation. At some stage, as we know, he decided to move to Iceland, and that changed his life. You've also relocated, and I'm curious to know what that means to you: was it an act of liberation? You're originally from Stuttgart, and now you live and work between Frankfurt and London. What's the relationship between the two cities, London and Frankfurt?

NH: Is Frankfurt the new Iceland?

AB: No, because Iceland was far removed from the art world. I don't think there was an interview marathon on Iceland while Roth was there! London is where my colleagues and the workshops are, that's more where my social life is based, and it's also more social as far as my work is concerned. Here in Frankfurt I have more peace and quiet. Sometimes that can be great and sometimes it can be uninspiring. There's a somatic difference between the two places: when I arrive at the airport in London I notice that I'm more alert.

HUO: What's your relationship to Frankfurt? I mean, this is where we really have to ask the Frankfurt question. What needs to change here? What annoys you about Frankfurt? What does Frankfurt lack? What's missing in Frankfurt? Is Frankfurt still modern? Let's talk about Frankfurt!

Brücken zur Literatur, so dass man sagen kann, dass er genauso Dichter, wie Schriftsteller und bildender Künstler war und außerdem eben sehr oft mit anderen Künstlern zusammengearbeitet hat.

AB: Und mit der Familie.

HUO: Mit der Familie, mit seinem Sohn Björn und mit einer Menge verschiedener Leute. Wir haben noch nicht darüber gesprochen, ob es Zusammenarbeit mit anderen Feldern gibt, ob du mit Wissenschaftlern oder mit Dichtern zusammenarbeitest.

AB: Ich hatte jetzt eine Zusammenarbeit mit Menschen aus verschiedenen Feldern, vor allem mit Künstlern, die ich um Instruktionen gebeten habe, wie man etwas fallen lassen kann. Dabei habe ich nicht nur Künstler gefragt, sondern auch Kuratoren und eine Schriftstellerin. Es war interessant, dass die jeweiligen Antworten, also die Instruktionen, die mir gegeben wurden, von den jeweiligen Disziplinen, geprägt waren. Jetzt fällt mir auf, dass es doch noch eine Zusammenarbeit mit Kuratoren gibt: Ich mache nämlich Interviews. In diesen Interviews befrage ich Kritiker oder Kuratoren als seien sie die Künstler. Das ist eine Zusammenarbeit, die ich mit anderen Disziplinen mache.

HUO: Du hast Instruktionen zum Fallenlassen erarbeitet. Führt das zu einem Film oder zu einem Buch?

AB: Nein, das ist eine Ausstellung. Also die Installation der Ausstellung, das heißt also die Aufbauzeit verbringe ich mit dem Fallenlassen, und die Spuren sind dann die Arbeit.

HUO: Eine Frage vielleicht noch zum Ortswechsel: Ich habe ein Interview gelesen mit Dieter Roth, da spricht er über diese Wichtigkeit des Ortswechsels. Irgendwann ist er ja nach Island gegangen. Das hat sein Leben verändert. Bei dir gibt es ja auch Ortswechsel. Ich bin neugierig, was der Ortswechsel für dich bedeutet: War das ein Befreiungsschlag? Du kommst ja aus Stuttgart und deine Städte

AB: Well, I like the Euro monument here behind us. I hope it stays. Hopefully it'll stay even if the European Central Bank leaves. Frankfurt lacks 2 million people. But still, I do also know a few people here that I'm happy to be with.

HUO: Thank you very much indeed, Andrea Büttner.

The interview was conducted as part of *The Frankfurt Conversation* at Schauspiel Frankfurt on 30 January 2011. *The Frankfurt Conversation* was a project by Städelschule and Portikus for the Frankfurter Positionen 2011.

1

In Anja Casser/Badischer Kunstverein, eds., *Andrea Büttner: I believe every word you say,* argobooks, Berlin, 2009.

2

'Artists at Work: Andrea Büttner', *Afterall Online*, http://www.afterall.org/online/artists. at.workandreabttner.

sind jetzt eben Frankfurt und London. Wie ist das Verhältnis zwischen den beiden Städten, London und Frankfurt?

NH: Ist Frankfurt dabei das neue Island?

AB: Nein, weil Island ganz weit weg von der Kunstwelt gewesen ist. Ich glaube, es gab keinen Interview-Marathon auf Island als Roth dort war. In London sind meine Kollegen und die Werkstätten, da habe ich eher mein soziales Leben; also auch beruflich sozialer. Und hie rin Frankfurt habe ich eher meine Ruhe. Diese Ruhe ist manchmal super und manchmal auch uninspirierend. An diesen unterschiedlichen Orten zu sein, ist ein somatischer Unterschied: Wenn ich am Flughafen in London ankomme, merke ich, dass ich wacher bin.

HUO: Wie ist dein Verhältnis zu Frankfurt? Ich meine, wir müssen hier unbedingt die Frankfurt-Frage stellen. Was sollte sich hier verändern, was ärgert dich in Frankfurt, was braucht Frankfurt, was fehlt in Frankfurt, ist Frankfurt noch modern? Let's talk about Frankfurt!

AB: Also ich mag dieses Euro-Denkmal hier hinter uns. Ich hoffe, dass es bleibt. Ich hoffe, dass es bleibt, auch wenn die Europäische Zentralbank von hier wegzieht. Frankfurt fehlen zwei Millionen Menschen. Ja, aber ein paar, mit denen ich glücklich bin, kenne ich doch auch hier.

HUO: Vielen, vielen Dank Andrea Büttner.

Das Interview wurde am 30. Januar 2011 bei den *Frankfurter Gesprächen* im Schauspiel Frankfurt geführt. Die *Frankfurter Gespräche* waren ein Projekt von Städelschule und Portikus im Rahmen der Frankfurter Positionen 2011

1

Anja Casser/Badischer Kunstverein (Hg.), *Andrea Büttner. I believe every word you say,* Berlin 2009.

2

Afterall online: Artists at Work: Andrea Büttner. <http://www.afterall.org/online/artists.at.workandreabttner>

I want to let the work fall down, 2005, woodcut, 99 × 140 cm

I want to let the work fall down

I want ornaments on everything, 2005, woodcut, 99 × 140 cm

I want ornaments on everything

Grid, 2012, woodcut, 115 × 173 cm

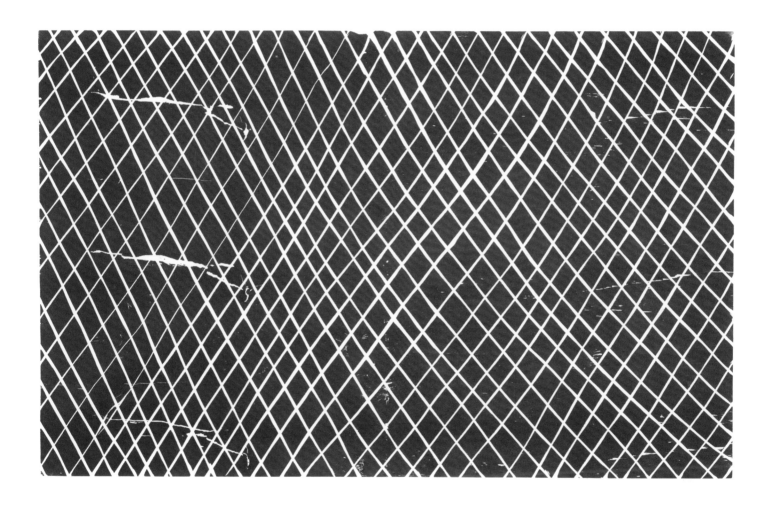

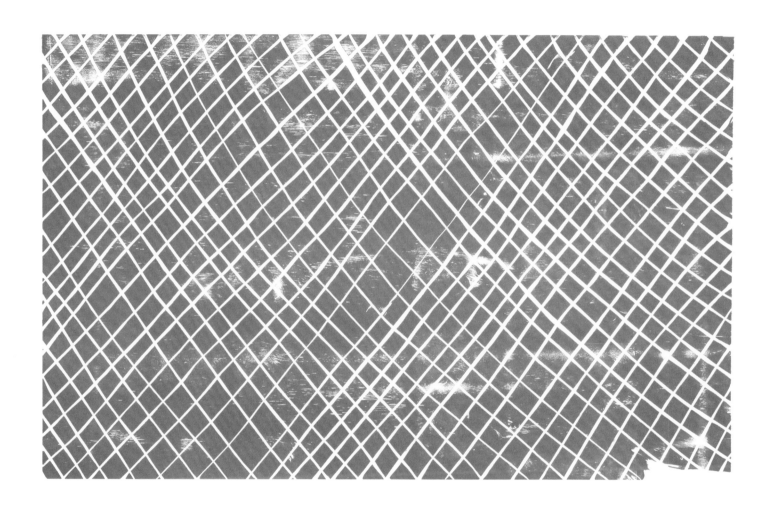

D. Roth and M. Kippenberger are meeting at the bridge of sighs, 2006,
woodcut, 60 × 30 cm

Roth Reading, 2006
Transcript of *Roth Reading*, 2006,
a 41-minute sound piece in
which all passages on shame and
embarrassment in Dieter Roth's
*Ein Tagebuch (aus dem Jahre
1982) / A Diary (from the year
1982)*, Reykjavik/Basel, 1984, are
recited.

[Roth's punctuation, syntax (such as the
successions of words trying to find the
right expression), and the misspellings
are an important feature of the text and
are kept intact in the sound piece.]

Foreword for the edition at the exhibition
„von hier aus" at Düsseldorf 1984:
here should be written about art, how
ashamed I feel about it (whether good
art or bad art), and about everything
connected...., but a big depression –
it has lasted, so far, for 2 years (?) – that
sits in me does keep me from writing
anything clearly about this art thing.

(At Staib & Mayer, printers)
I feel a slight shame how I get myself to
act friendly.

I have moments when say: „To flatter
openly (even if detectable to the person
I flatter, not only the reader or specta-
tor), simply do it!" Writing this I feel how
little I do show, lay open, and today, the
1. of April I feel: When I write „lay open"
I mean to lay open events or feelings
that I ordinarily am ashamed to show,
but as soon as I try to show it, it appears
harmless, cute.

shyness, not to be able to show off
in Italian…I hope people do not hear
my German accent when speaking
English or French.

In the pavillion I want to leave the
slightly dirty walls as they are, Godoni
says – after I had said – „C'est la vie"–:
„Monsiuer Roth dit: „C'est la vie." I then
feel shame, think of this often the next
days and first about 2 days I find the
sentence (after about 2 days): „The dirt
and also the other things that „disturb"
you – just clean it and take them away–
C'est la vie, aussi." I say this solution
(sol for me) – sentence, during the following week to everybody i give this story.
I say in addition: „I wished I had thought
of it already when I answered Godoni."

I fear to see her body clearly (make
me a picture of her body by looking at it
intensely), because then I would try to
push aside my timidity (~~that keeps both~~
(does this timidity hold both of us back?)
I feel at least shame over my body.
(Gertrud has talked about my being fat
several times) I cannot touch her,
as earlier, trusting that she will find me
exciting, too.
    I give up to write about this timidity-
theme, I fear she will not like this when
she reads it (imagine arguments).

Do not dare to do filming there
[at Tomas Schmit's home] (fear, to be
thought of as too selfconscious, exag-
gerated?) Hear myself say sentences
wherein parts reflect other parts (?) and
am ashamed (every time when I hear
myself say sentences wherein I appear
to give thoughts about parts of these
sentences (?), why am I ashamed of
that? ashamed, also, every time I make
sentences especially for Tomas' (ear)
(understanding (?) – arranging them
partly with what I see as his vocabulary.

I call Dorothy to speak to Rainer Pretzell.
I promise, timidly, to Dorothy to meet
her. (Did not keep the promise – fear and
ashamed the whole next day about this)

The couples on the (symmetrical) drawings become increasingly homosexual,
especially the dogs, dancing in front of
each other, they have been changed into
men that make each other come (fountains). Of this I would have been shy not
more than a year ago.

Since always on short trips (all the time)
and short stays and short periods of
feeling erotic (excited) or euphoric, do
almost never find anybody to make
rendezvous´. Those few (rendezv.) that
I make I make weakly-timidly, so that I can
give in to weak moods and stay away
without having to be ashamed.

Increasing self-fear and -anger, while
thinking of how I can keep up this way of
living if I can sell quickly made stuff
expensively – an old kind of moral fear.
[„fear" = „Scham"!]

[After cleaning the kitchen:] I say to
myself so often, I wish to be able to stand
disorder much better and I imagine me
„tolerating easily disorder as well as dirt
without getting into conditions of fear
or shame."

I cannot stand anymore (for two years
now, at least) the music that I listened
to with tears in my eyes (still, sometimes
I cry with music when drunk).
    When listening I picture for myself
the music making machinery, keeping
busy tough and patient and healthy but
hard, ambitious people that do not like
me. Remember discussions with pro-
fessional musicians, read and heard
interviews of the keepers and executives
of the established music scene, my fear,
from early times of my live on, compare
them with myself, imagine how I look like
one of them and become ashamed. But
I cannot comfort myself with the results
of my own efforts in that field, in such
moments I look at them as the products
of resentment.

When I watched lemon pressing in Paris
(while putting up my exhibition in at the
gallery Bama: „Theses small, slim, nimble
French…" I often said, but afterwards
I thought: „These are Parisians only; even
only 10 or 12 peoplethat I have seen,
in the centre of Paris (around the Seine).

On the 15th of April I say: „Painful bla
bla!" – and this sentence (of the 12th of
Apr.) works (on the 15th of A.) painful
on me, and this („painful on me") painful
[embarrassing] o. m.

Reading Bernhard Luginbühl´s „The
Small Explosive Kitchen" in a copy
I bought after I had forgotten to take the
copy in which Bernhard had written
a dedication with me from Mötschwil,
where the Luginbühls live. Feel ashamed
(about the forgotten book). I ask, while
writing the word „ashamed", what I want
to say, to whom I want to talk, and I tell
myself: it seems I want to counteract the
impression I fear to have made when
I left the book behind. – When somebody
leaves behind at my place something
I have given, I become angry – sad each
time. Recently I started to feel ashamed
to have pushed the present onto the
guest, especially if the guest has not
asked for the object or begged for it.

At Holderbank I cannot decide how to
do the films, I am insecure since
I feel Bernhard has expected better
technic and extensive preparations on
my side (I had called, when I asked
him for permission, this affair an this
meeting an interview). Some shame
while unpacking the camera, growing
shame while i listen to my questions –
I have never had the opportunity to
talk to people I admire – that is envy –,
or whom I wished to be my friends, and
to whom I rather would like to talk
about anxieties and fears then about
work and fun, never been talking to
them while both were using the same
language: Their mothertongue. (English
works (best) second best?) Swiss
German I can speak without shyness
only when drunk.

In Basel 1/2 18 meet Tadeus Pfeiffer at
restaurant „St. Alban Stübli". He wants
to interview me for the „Brückenbauer"
(newspaper). I stick to mineral water
(1 hour?) then wine. He is a drinker (I can
see after a while), and we go to another
restaurant, fairly heavy drinking. Talk:
both give in to my tendency to pronounce
complaints to complain. I cannot break
this, my shame mourning all the time.
At the hotel angry to myself while waiting
for the expected hangover to start.

On my way, highway to Solothurn and
Basel, I am not sure whether I should
turn off to Gerlafingen: The stay in
G. – already imagining it – too difficult
because mother lives there. I have not
visited her so long and I have not written
to her so long that I get from her the
most sad letters, and I do not answer
for months and years. If I have not
answered a letter from her for 1-2
months, I cannot overcome my inhibition
to write to her. I retire into stubborn-
ness: „I only get sad letters, that shall
make me write out of fear to get
sad letters. So I pass Gerlafingen most
often, shame, spite, anger mounting
further each time.

To Basel to be in time for dinner with the Rembrandt-Award committee and Emmett Williams and Tomas Schmit. Apprehensions of the evening and the dinner – how to get through the evening without too much drinking, so that I am not depressed the next day (when the award will be handed to me), and stage-fright will not bother me extraordinary (because hang over)?

Dinner with the committee, I eat little and drink, to start with, mineral water, but cannot keep this up (appear boring to myself, fear to appear boring to others), I go on drinking wine, whiskey. Drunk, I draw on several napkins, different subjects, to excite the female members of the group. Am irritated that they do not take this straight (they don't take it seriously, meant to be excite them sexually). All go – except Emmett, Tomas and Barbara – at 11 h. I want to order more wine, but the waitresses say there is no more wine. This I take as I took such situations many years ago (20–30?), th. is, I get angry and talk, shout, something about injustice and „to leave me, the award winner, like that!" But feel ashamed of this. No memory to write down (the 9th of may) what happened after that shouting.

Around 17.00 we go to Emmett's room, whiskey, beer. Can not get ourselves to move and go to the celebration. We get there though, but too late. I am neither ashamed nor feel stagefright. Emmett's speech (we are at the art museum) makes me feel moved about myself, in a new way that… (I cannot read what followed here – today the 17th April 1984)) the listeners disappear from my consciousness, not even one of the main fears [: how can Tomas stand this oldfashioned ways of living without detesting me (the one that takes it all, enjoying it immoderately)] comes up. The president of the award committee calls my answer „not nice" (I simply said „Good bye" 2 times) and used this remark to become angry and go away.

I think at the moment of many scenes in concerts with Ossi Wiener, Gerhard Rühm, Hermann Nitsch, Brus, Attersee or with Arnulf Rainer, and I think of the "Kümmerling Sonata"-LP. I feel very uneasy when I listen to or look at recordings of these scenes when I see myself appearing as what Renate Steiger once called my authoritarian attitude. But mostly I get comfort – when I am ashamed as described – with by comparison, I look at performances of others whom I do not look at as disgusting (at least, not anything disgusting that disgusts me), they do take the view (or the sound) of themselves more or less badly, too. Then I tell myself: Your fear consists surely in fearing to appear as displeasing to others as you appear to yourself, but the others are not ambitious for your benefit (but for their own). They do not suffer from unfulfilled ambition (regarding appearance) in your affairs, but, the most, in their affairs.

Such sentences give relieve only for seconds. Disgust of self goes on after the shortest interval, especially strong when weak after several drinking days.

Guests at Ursula's. I fight with Hans Saner (stilisticly, my stile our arguments like those I used 30 years ago, i think.) He says things like: „This simply is no good!" – when I say a poem for instance. I try to outdo smart him with the listeners with poems I learned as a boy in the street, at Hannover, very strong stuff (poetically and dirtily) I know, - and I say I can remember 100 poems (4 lines each), but I only know at the 10. Feel being cruel, shame according.

On such a day (after several days of drinking) I stay in bed, for further 2 days, at least – but only when I am alone. When in company, I feel ashamed and stay „on my feet".

When we arrive in Stuttgart I show to Emmett parts of the heap, made up of my A4 (format) drawings-books. I have come to see (in the last years more and more), that this is an imposing activity, so this time I do not stay with Emmett (to look, too). I say to Emmett, I want to give him one of the books as a birthday-present. I believe to feel, how heavy presents become, th. i. they work like a burden as a burden. [The mechanism of this, I want to give something that reminds the receiver of me as a master or somebody like that (in a certain field), for a long time]. Often I give such object to people that are bound to get the feeling they will never be able to do such things make such stuff themselves – so this weighs on them. Already 3-4 times recipients weight back to me; they simply said or written something that made clear what mechanism was at work in the transaction., and I, easy to understand, was ashamed, I suffer, in such cases, from never to alleviate shame (at the moment not to alleviate, as the most: to forget, slowly): There are a (very) few persons to whom I do not dare to give presents (of my work), I know they know how the mechanics of present weighing works. – Or I know that my books or pictures don't tell them anything like relieve or entertainment; they see through my presents, th. is through my products: see ambition or moneymaking (the wish to make money or the necessity to make money). Tendencies that keep the pictures (for instance) on the level of the easily acceptable, which for those persons lays too low, holds too little objectives that interests them. Or maybe they see the melancholic fight, the self-satisfying selfdissatisfying, always humourless **effort**; this effort can bring humouristic **products** – though humour on an effortless level, on which one will not find, while living on it (that level) any humour, not even irony. So there „gibt's nichts zu lachen" (there are no laughs to find) – for these connaisseurs.

In Berlin I went to see Y. [I had felt for years she did not want to be intimate with me. When we met the last year before this time, I found she had thought the same (about me).] This time, in spite of much drinking (both), we do not become near get near nor excited, verbally. The words with which she invited me to bed, late (I had not dared to say anything like that) were said matter of fact way, so the transition to body-nearness was (for my abilities) not decorous or fussy enough, and i did not get an erection; too ashamed to talk about lack of intimate-excitement-talk, even too ashamed to simply to mention that) Am relieved that both say, we have to meet, ???? some people.

I invite him [Rainer] and Agnes for dinner. We go to the Yugoslaw restaurant near Stresemannstrasse. I am tired and depressed and try calm talk, but do not succeed. Tempted to complain, much stuff complainable comes to my mind. I feel relieved (which is rare) that Rainer has no talent for listening to complainty gossip or for comforting me, I feel relieved since I would have to become ashamed, always to talk about my defeats and losses, that do not happen, exist, in other people's eyes, that see incomparable much for success with me.

Wolfgang Wunderlich comes to fetch pictures for an exhibition at Klewan gallery (1 month later) in München Munic. He drives me (his wife Susanne stays, to wait, at her mother's house) to Wendelin Niedlich's house, to get the pictures there, that Wendelin had had in consignment, standing on the floor or hanging on the walls, of the flat; i am slightly ashamed to take them away, justify with talk about „we two having nothing flourishing going anyway "or„ I really need some money awfully! "But Niedlich is sad, nevertheless, and on top of that has been, the same day, at the dentist for a big operation, and he is sick, cannot move his mouth, lips, when he wants to smile, I feel cruel when I see that he cannot well smile when I talk calembours (to hide my guilt) feelings while taking the pictures away.

I fear the Stuttgarter registration office: From 1972–1981 i believed (since i was not registered) that the registration people would find out, catch me, in case i had a street accident or raise the attention of the police in other ways. So i drove, since the time i got a car in Germany (Switzerland), 1977, carefully, not to be noticed (though i had on my car a customs' number, and later a Swiss number). I said to myself: „If those fellows stop me and ask, where do you live, and i say, i live in Switzerland, and they ask, What do you do here in Stuttgart? – Oh, I am only visiting. And if they then had asked: Where do you stay? – Then I would not have liked to give them up Uwe Lohrer's address, he (Uwe) must not get into disagreable things situations by my doings. I, on the other hand, fear, in such imagined talks or questionings, to give the address of my Danneckerstrasse flat, since, then „They would have got the idea, that i live there unregistered!" Such sentences (of fear) and such discussions (imagination or fear) become especially disturbing (hightened anxiety) when hungover. In the winter of 1981/82 I talked to the lawyer Mayer-Rosa, in Stuttgart, and since that talk I am calm; just sometimes I get angry or ashamed about or of those more than 10 years I was afraid of the registr. people, without knowing that I was free to live in Stuttgart (as Swiss person) without registering.

On the trips to Wangen where Kodak's factory (films to process) each time (i am) in the worst mood; Think of how show to how i show in front of Bö. this dissatisfied forth-and-back-life, and how i pull him into it, too. Am ashamed how I tell, justifying talk, about „to have to make money – somehow" plus „nowhere as well possible as here (Germany and Switzerl.)" I ask myself how much I have infected him already (Vera, Karl, too)?

This morning with Emil Wartmann in the railstation-restaurant, we make a list of the stuff to put on the show. The pleasure to see the (mostly old work) pictures and sculpt.'s again and a certain pride („nobody has done this yet!") do not get me but of the constant melancholia. To start with, Björn makes the films, but i beg him to go on filming in the station (we were at the storeroom) – am ashamed of the show of „The crazy ambitionist" that i feel myself playing for him. (?)

some several kinds of fear on railroad stations
The fear, to have some or all these fears for nothing (the feared circumstances or events will not become reality). Out of these and similar feelings come up especially clear sentences, spoken to myself: „This timid dog!" „This disgustingly timid self-troublemaker" „this one is stands again in his own way!" When I say such these sentences to myself, i seem to get relieve from those fears i am scolding me for;
especially while writing these sentences, today, in the Swiss pavillon of the Biennale area in Venice, (the 7th of June ´82) – but i only get relieve while writing, - not while reading and re-reading. [I cannot stand it, to read the text of this catalogue (i read it with disgust or shame, though sometimes slight) after writing, at least for the time being. Other texts i have not been able to read could not stand to read for several months. Like pictures, most of them I cannot look at (after they have come to an advanced stage) for a long time, those who appear most disgusting to me i do not look at two, sometimes three years. In this case they seem to me (especially clearly when i show them to somebody as things, mishappened but to be shown bravely) suddenly (?), often, as something brave, and finished, luckily.

Today, looking down at the churchyard, i see peolple sprinkling water on graves and pray, and i prepare, automatically (i do this always? for 10 years now?), arguments of defense, against christian claims that i feel often subjected to when i look or listen to christian ceremonials – even if the cerm. is happening on a picture.

To start with (first argument): „The superstition of these people one could compare (for them), or it could be explained (to them), with the superstition of the so-called (by them so called) primitive people – both wear ornaments (cloths and move ornamentally. The „primitive" (called) peoples' superstition cannot be differentiated from the superstition of the Christian people." Then (a later argument), since i cannot exept myself easily from being superstitious, i talk to myself like this: „with me, it is the belief in superstition (believing there exists supersition) that is the superstition." and then: „To say, there exist superstition, is a symptom of sickness, the sickness one calls superstition." Then, after that, I often say – in rather quiet times: „Belief one could call superstition and superstition one can call belief." But this sounds so banal, that my shame wants me to find some other way out of it, then i say sentences like this: „Names one can call things!" – then, mostly, i fall back on the small fears that i had before i started on that chain of sentences.– Here in Mols that is the fear of the people in the churchyard, who can watch my house and see we have no curtains, and can critizise me, us on it.

We drive to Bern, with the pages of the Bienn. cata. that are ready for printing and i want to bring to Dr. Menz. […] I show to Bö. where i have lived, slight shame as i listen to myself talk about how poor i was, how much we drank, what company we were, for, if other people talk about such facts i feel bothered: „And here i passed every day …", „there, in that corner i sat…" etc. So i am tempted to talk about the places (they have changed) and their actual look and function negatively; this i do haltingly (according to the mentioned shame), and this way of speaking depresses me so, that i do not find many of the (Icelandic) words i find, ordinarily, – augmented shame.
In the rest. Zähringer the terrace is almost fully occupied, we sit down inside – i suggest this, talking around the right reason for my wish (shy in places full of people) and saying: „The sun is shining too strongly, outside – for my feeling." – I should have declared this as a side-feeling, but, declaring it a main-feeling,my shame mounts, I become restless and have to try white wine in bettering my mood and the talking. This disturbs a certain mood that i have been building up, for some days, by alcohol abstinence, bettering, for some days while not drinking.

The next day we drive to the repair-service place of the Braun people (cameras). It comes to my mind that we have neither seen nor heard any of the films taken until now. Since February the camery seems to work too loudly (in my ears); i fear one will hear these over-sounds when we project the films later. Though is say to myself once again those sentences of „Everything shall be allowed, failure too!", i succeed in calming me only for seconds.

The camera - engineer at Braun becomes suspicious when he sees me filming (especially when i film his hands, and i talk confusedly to detratct his attention, i feel shame for this. Björn asks, what happens? (He has registered the knots in my talk with the ingeneer). I say something about suspicion, in Icelandic, to Björn; but am afraid, suddenly, of the engineer suspecting us to try to hide from him a (bad for him) secret, so I try to translate the Islandic sentences into German, but feel i should not translate simply „he has become suspicious", but have to say or should say something quite innocent. I say it – the gestures and the tone of voice are surely innocent enough, but the expression of my face must be one of somebody caught.

I wanted to film out of all windows, all around out of the house, but was afraid to film out of some windows – against the light. In the disorder of our days' programm, daily life, i did not get myself later to film at least out of some windows, with the light, where in the morning the films would have been taken against th. l. I asked Vera to make the films (the films I did not make); I told myself: If i do not tell her that I was afraid to work against the light, she will surely do it, without hesitation – simply to make what I ordered. But a slight shyness brought me to telling her of my hesitation in front of that light.

The feeling, i infect Björn and Vera with my pessimistic moods, every morning, give them certain anxieties. Although I have been able to stop cursing (about life) 2–3 years ago (with people present, in the mornings); in the evenings, when drunk f.inst., I still am giving rough, ugly sentences to people that seem to have given me cause. The next day I am much ashamed, more or less – according to the degree of my hangover.
In Zug we put up bank accounts for Vera & Björn. Luckily I have still got some money, at least I can pay, what I owe them, into their accounts (around 3000,– SFR). Slightly angry at myself when I watch me having the usual (for 20 years now?) fear of the teller (maybe rather to call shame (instead of fear), since it only appears when I ask for the usual small figures i have to do with, or when I ask what I have got on my account (there is usually very little – a few thousand, undeten, only). The teller seems timid to me, he does not seem to be able to decide which

language to speak with me (Bö., Vera & I talk Icelandic), and I feel relieved from my timidity in front of him, that I have felt for the last 2–3 years.

One could call this room a D.R.-room, since there Sohm collects my small pictures since 1962(?). Almost all these pictures were failures, in my eyes, at the time i made them, – some are unfinished. Framed (by H.S. most of them) they look better then the pictures i called good (at that time). Though, these pictures here look like p's out of the nineteenth century, and I can only look at them when in my best (bodily speaking) condition, without becoming mixed up between anger and shame.

Late we drive to Basel, should take a double room in hotel Euler, no rooms else unoccupied. Both are shy, though; I call A. whether I can sleep with her. To start with sexually well excited and erection, but I do not undress and talk a long time, until I begin to listen to myself, talking, ashamed (of the commonplace stuff), and my erection is since only good for fucking shortly, but then shame again, about the talk (my talk) that I use to gloss over failing erection.

From then on i did not only work sporadically for Gudmundur Kristinsson (the architect), but got work from him to take home, building models of some of his houses. In this connection i got to know the manager of a paintfactory, who lent me the money for the ticket to New York, in 1958 (the first try to get work in another country), but after 6 months of difficulties in Philadelphia & New York i came, ashamed, back to R'vk.

Great difficulties to pay the house. She [Roth's wife] sold it in 1981. I envy her for the strength to let go an object that has cost one several years of great effort. My ambitions have never allowed me (or shame has prevented me) to give up, or only draw back, in other peoples' sight. The larger part of my efforts has got its impetus anyway only out of reluctance to give in (reluctance to give up), - still is getting it therefrom. I have not been able yet to change that (do I wish to change it?).

But he did not find the money, so, to feel constantly in need for money (i did not make enough then) and to make a constant and exhausting effort to get hold of money got me to feel tense and tired, my patience gave away, friendship suffered. 2 or 3 years after buying it we went, for the last time together, to the house, and Ragnar said goodbye. We since have only met once, but i could not see whether he was still sad or had come over this. My shame was constantly intense and has kept me away from him.

I was shy to be discovered as foreigner […] and so i did not stay inside these houses, stopped to get petrol only.

They [Agnar Gustafsson and his wife Inga Dora Hertevig] have a weekend house in the east of Reykjavik, with many horses around, by a little lake. When I visited there some years ago we drank white wine the hosts had made from I did not know what, and it tasted good (I am not such a small drinker), not easily to recognice as artificial. There were visitors from Germany and we german speakers talked a lot. I was ashamed (a little) how loud we were or how nervous – compared to Agmar's quiet (easily envied by me, too).

Books by artists that have been given or sent (because I had participated) to me. These books I rarely am able to look into – beside the books of a few good friends (colleagues). I am reluctant to keep only the books (out of fear of shame?) that I like. So I not only keep them because they are dedicated to me or because I have got them from the authors, but because the bulk of the collection would look poor without them (all). At all the places I have lived, I have the same fear: If I only keep what appears useful (instruments, objects) and what appears interesting (works), the whole would look poor (writing of the imagined impression the impression I imagine they make on others) – to myself they look the stuff that is lying about, standing up collected, sadly.

But to use these presses I do not have the patience anymore (I am spoiled, printed so many years with masters of the craft), and I do not feel driven anymore to use these old technics: 1) I have not built up any sales-medium for my prints, so I do – after many rows with dealers – not sell almost any prints any more. 2) the dirty, impatient, fast way of making my paintings I cannot go an these old presses – seems to me (or, only with a certain measure of order and patience)! […]
    In this way I feel burdened, see useless heaps of machinery pile up. I feel anger and shame. (Shame in front of imagined people that see through the efficiency – that I am playacting – into my inefficiency. Such shame overcomes me especially strongly when I am working at getting the presses through customs or while transport (from the harbour) is going on. I then feel built into a ridiculously small but deadly machine, I feel my life disppearing in this machinery-action.

The friendship cools down, I feel ashamed, I suspect myself to have acted to act cruelly, I constantly have to work to take the edge off this suspicion, I repress my shame.

Corita Reading, 2006
Transcript of *Corita Reading*, 2006, a 42-minute sound piece based on texts quoted by Sister Corita Kent in her serigraphs.[1]

song about the greatness, 1964
Let the ocean thunder with all its waves the world and all who dwell there. The rivers clap their hands, the mountains shout together with joy before the Lord, for he comes.[2]

wide open, 1964
Open wide…that the King of Glory may enter in.[3]
Open wide the exits from poverty to the children of the poor.[4]

the juiciest tomato of all, 1964
The time is always out of joint…If we are provided with a sign that declares "Del Monte tomatoes are juiciest," it is not desecration to add: "Mary Mother is the juiciest tomato of them all." Perhaps this is what is meant when the slang term puts it, "She's a peach," or "What a tomato!" A cigarette commercial states: "So round, so firm, so fully packed" and we are strangely stirred, even ashamed as we are to be so taken in. We are not taken in. We yearn for the fully packed, the circle that is so juicy and perfect that not an ounce more can be added. We long for the "groaning board," the table overburdened with good things, so much we can never taste, let alone eat, all there is. We long for the heart that overflows for the all-accepting of the bounteous, of the real and not synthetic, for the armful of flowers that continues the breast, for the fingers that make a perfect blessing.

There is no irreligiousness in joy, even if joy is pump-primed at first. Someone must enter the circle first, especially since the circle appears menacing. The fire must be lit, a lonely task, then it dances. The spark of flame teaches one person to dance and that person teaches others, and then everyone can be a flame. Everyone can communicate. But someone must be burned. Perhaps everyone who would participate entirely in the dance must have some part of himself burned, and may shrink back. They look for some familiar action to relate to. There is too yawning a gulf between oneself and the spirit, so we turn to our supermarkets, allegories; a one-to-one relationship. You pay your money, you get your food, you eat it, it's gone. But intangibly, during the awkward part of the dance, with the whole heart not in it, with the eye furtively looking out for one's own ridiculousness, allegory becomes symbol, wine becomes blood, wafer flesh and the spark flames like bright balloons released, and the "heart leaps up to behold," and somehow we have been taken from the greedy signs of barter and buying, from supermarket to supermundane. We have proceeded from the awkward to the whole. The rose of all the world becomes, for awhile, and in our own terms, the "pause that refreshes," and possibly what was a pause becomes the life.[5]

tender be – part one – sr. william, 1964
So yes, I think Mary laughed out loud – she laughed wholeheartedly, without rancor, and with great compassion, and with real reverence. If she were here today in her physical nature she would surely laugh. She would laugh at our wreaths; she would laugh at our pop art; she would laugh – compassionately – at the consternation of some of us at this riot of sound and color, at our uncertainty about its suitability for a day of religious celebration. Frankly, I think Mary would want this day, that she would like to think that it was well explained by calling it her day. She is the cause of our joy – and I hope that we bring her joy by praising her with our hearts on high. If we were only loud and bright, perhaps we could hope only for the indulgent smile of the mother of very small children. Our colors, however are the colors of the marketplace, the colors of life-giving food, and our sounds are the sounds of the here and now, and they are meant to say: mother, I am concerned for my brother, who is your son.

My brother starves, he weeps, he dies. He is myself. Today is a loud call to our mother asking her to teach us what she knows of filling the emptiness, drying the tears, and easing the death of our brother. We ask to be taken out of ourselves (this is the whole burden of "Pacem in Terris").[6]

tender be – part two – sr. william, 1964
Rest at pale evening…
A tall, slim tree…
Night coming tenderly
Black like me.[7]

I am the man, I suffer'd, I was there….
I am the hounded slave, I wince at the bite of the dogs …
I do not ask the wounded person how he feels, I myself become the wounded person….
All these I feel or am.[8]

mary does laugh, 1964
Mary does laugh, and she sings and runs and wears bright orange. Today she'd probably do her shopping at the Market Basket.[9]

someday is now, 1964
America's experience is that social concern itself is inevitable. Responsibility for one another is what we mean when we say we are one nation under God.[10]

I have a dream that one day every valley shall be exalted, every hill and mountain shall be made low, the rough places will be made plain, and the crooked places will be made straight, and the glory of the Lord shall be revealed, and all flesh shall see it together.[11]

enriched bread, 1965
Great ideas, it has been said, come into the world as gently as doves. Perhaps then, if we listen attentively, we shall hear, amid the uproar of empires and nations, a faint flutter of wings, the gentle stirring of life and hope. Some will say that this hope lies in a nation; others, in a man. I believe rather that it is awakened, revived, nourished by millions of solitary individuals whose deeds and works every day negate frontiers and the crudest implications of history. As a result, there shines forth fleetingly the ever threatened truth that each and every man, on the foundation of his own sufferings and joys, builds for all.[12]

my people, 1965
The body of Christ is no more comfortable now than it was when it hung from the cross.

Those who live in the well organized, well ordered, nourished, clean, calm and comfortable middle-class part of Christ's body can easily forget that the body of Christ, as it now exists, is mostly disorganized, devoid of order, concerned with the material needs, hungry, dirty, not motivated by reason, fermenting in agonizing uncertainty and certainly most uncomfortable.

Youth is a time of rebellion. Rather than squelch the rebellion, we might better enlist the rebels to join that greatest rebel of his time – Christ himself.[13]

bread breaking, 1965
When I hear bread breaking I see something else; it seems almost as though God never meant us to do anything else. So beautiful a sound, the crust breaks up like manna and falls all over everything, and then we eat; bread gets inside humans.[14]

people like us yes, 1965[15]

power up, 1965
God has chosen his mother to put an end to all distance. The first choice of Christians is Christ. Where is your brother? Want nothing small about men. Except maybe their words, which should be modest and thoughtful and almost inaudible before their DEEDS. For the rest, bigness; heart, brain; Imagination too; let it take the world in two hands and show us what it's like to BE! Tell us about it, we're hungry. Doesn't the Bible call truth BREAD? We're starved, our smile has lost out, we crawl around on a thin margin – a life, maybe, but what for? And who wants it anyway?

Where's the man who says yes, and says no, like a thunderclap? Where's the man whose no turns to yes in his mouth – he can't deny life, he asks like a new flower or a new day or a hero even; what more is there to love than I have loved?

When I hear bread breaking, I see something else; it seems almost as though god never meant us to do anything else. So beautiful a sound, the crust breaks like manna and falls all over everything, and then we EAT;

bread gets inside humans and turns into what the experts call "formal glory of god." But don't let that worry you. Sometime in your life, hope you might see one starved man, the look on his face when the bread finally arrives.

Hope you might have baked it or bought it or even needed it for yourself. For the look on his face for your hands meeting his across a piece of bread, you might be willing to lose a lot or suffer a lot – or die a little, even.

"Formal glory," well yes. Maybe what we're trying to understand is what they're trying to say, who knows? I don't think they understand – or every theologian would be working part time in a breadline. Who knows. Who might greet them there or how their words might change afterwards like stones into bread? Most theologians have never broken bread for anyone in their lives. Do you know, I think they think Christ is as well fed as his statues are?

But I don't know. Man keeps breaking in.

Take your "typical man" across the world. Let him in. Look at him, he isn't white, he probably isn't clean. He certainly isn't fed or American, or Catholic. So then what? What's left? Well, maybe now we're getting somewhere; Christ is ALL that's left if you're looking for a mystery. He's real as a man. Don't just stand there! Sit him down. Offer him some bread! He'll understand that; bread comes across. So does Christ; Luke says so – in the breaking of the bread. What a beautiful sound – try and see!

I keep thinking of that poor man. And his face, when someone on earth shows up against all odds to treat him like a human being. But that isn't all, or even half the truth. The half, or more, is what he sees is you.

And that's a mercy, because Christ is merciless about the poor. He wants them around – always, and everywhere. He's condemned them to live with us. It's terrifying. I mean for us too. It's not only that we are ordered, rigorously ordered, to serve the poor. That's hard enough; Christ gives so few orders in all the gospel. But the point is, what the poor see in us – and don't see, too. We stand there, American, white, Catholic, with the keys of the kingdom and the keys of the world in our pocket. Everything about us says: Be like me! I've got it made. But the poor man sees the emperor – naked. Like the look of Christ, the poor man strips us down to the bone. And then if we're lucky something dawns – even on us.

Why, we're the poor. The reel plays backward, everything's reversed when the gospel is in the air. The clothes fly off Dives, he's negro, he's nothing, he's got his hand out forever. Empty as a turned up skull. Watch the reel now – it's important to see which way the

bread is passing. To you, to me! We're in luck. This is our day.

The poor have it hard, the saying goes. Well, we're the hardest thing they have. Do you know I think sometime if we poor rich are ever going to grow up into faith, it will only be because poor men are around – everywhere, always, everywhere, drunks, winos, junkeys, the defeated, the ne'er do wells, those who didn't make it on to our guarded spoiled playground. And those who never wanted to play our game and whose rags are therefore a kind of riches we will never wear. All of them, a special Providence, a holy rain and sun, falling equally on the unjust, the smooth con men, the well oiled Cadillac humans and inhumans, the purblind, those who made it, the Christians and their impure Gods in cupboards and banks and nuclear silos, the white unchristian west, all of us. Who but for the poor would never know who we are, or where we came from or where we are (just possibly) going – in spite of tons of catechisms and the ten editions of the Handbook for Instant Salvation and the best of sellers, I Kept You Know Who Out and Found god.

On the cloud of unknowing; hog Blind as bats. Then a poor man (they are all miracle men, they have to be to live one day in our world) stands there. His poverty is like a few loaves and fishes – enough for everyone!

He breaks and breaks bread and feeds us and we live up again and again literally bottomless with sour need, going for broke, sore and ill tempered and jostling one another, hearing the word pass down the line, there's hardly any left, resenting straining forward in a frenzy of despair. But there's always enough, always some more. Christ guarantees it – I Don't know why. The poor you have always with you. Like a marvelous legacy of god. His best possession, in our hands. Undeserved, like the Eucharist. O send someone in from the gate where Dives sits on a dungheap in his sores, send even one of the dogs to whimper for us – would Lazarus of his heart's goodness let a dog lick up the crumbs from the floor, and carry even in a dog's mouth something for the damned.

This is the truth about the world, our Lord said. Everything comes right, all the deep wrongs of existence are turned inside out, the rich are stripped even of their shrouds, the poor men go in wedding garments.

The first way to defeat Christianity is to strike the Christians blind. Let the rich really think they have made it and can hang on to it all, and wheeler deal even with the angel of judgement named Christ, and (imagine) face him for the first time in death – when all of life is a great tragic Greek chorale sung by Christs in masks, sometimes furies, sometimes racked women. Sometimes a foul wino in a pismire sings it out like a bird of paradise remembering his last incarnation, but never, never looks up when Mr. Big goes by. The

untranslated, unbearable unbearable cry, pure judgement, pure anger, pure rejection. Reality! Reality!

O the poor will line up before the Judge with Torrid Eyes, a handful of daisies in His right hand, a sword in the other. They look gently toward His right side. They know. Come. They were the workers of corporal mercy. They are saved for having been, for being, for being others.

They save even us.
They carried fresh bread to stale lives. Come, beloved of my Father.[16]

lesson nine, 1966
The sun is very full of sunshine which is very pleasant just at nine, when the wash is hanging out on the line. Turkeys are wild and turkeys are tame which is a shame. Peacocks too and they are blue and if all this is true who are you. This is what the sun said when after having been up since nine he thought of setting time after time, but they said no, what is there to show that the sun has sunshine if he is setting all the time. So the sun said he would shine even if it was nine and he did just as if he was a lid which he was because there was a cover which did cover all around the sun cover the sun all up and after that there was no bother nobody had to get up even at nine. Anyway there was no sunshine, not yesterday. It is different today. Thank you very much for such.[17]

stop the bombing, 1967
I am in Vietnam
who will console me?

I am terrified of bombs,
of cold wet leaves and bamboo splinters in my feet, of a bullet cracking through the trees, across the world, killing me – there is a bullet in my brain,
behind my eyes, so that all I see is pain

I am in Vietnam
who will console me?

from the six o'clock news,
from the headlines lurking on the street, between the angry love songs
on the radio,
from the frightened hawks
and angry doves I meet,
a war I will not fight is killing me –

I am in Vietnam
who will console me?[18]

greetings, 1967
When I hear bread breaking, I see something else; it seems almost as though God never meant us to do anything else. So beautiful a sound, the crust breaks like manna and falls all over everything, and then we eat; bread gets inside humans. Sometime in your life, hope you might see one starved man, the look on his face when the bread finally arrives. Hope you might have baked it or bought it or even needed it for your self. For the look on his face for your hands meeting his across a piece of bread, you

might be willing to lose a lot or suffer a lot – or die a little, even.[19]

right, 1967
And if only we arrange our life according to that principle which counsels us that we must always hold to the difficult, then that which now seems to us the most alien will become what we most trust and find most faithful. How should we be able to forget those ancient myths that are at the beginning of all peoples, the myths about dragons that at the last moment turn into princesses; perhaps all the dragons of our lives are princesses who are only waiting to see us once beautiful and brave. Perhaps everything terrible is in its deepest being something that wants help from us.[20]

somebody had to break the rules, 1967
The rose is a rose,
And was always a rose.
But the theory now goes
That the apple's a rose,
And the pear is, and so's
The plum, I suppose.
The dear only knows
What will next prove a rose.
You, of course, are a rose –
But were always a rose.[21]

fresh bread, 1967
A jug of wine a loaf of bread and WOW.[22]

What kind of a revolution would it be if all the people in the whole world would sit around in a circle and eat together?[23]

What you seek in vain for half your life, one day you come full upon, all the family at dinner.[24]

handle with care, 1967
no time ago
or else a life
walking in the dark
i met christ

jesus)my heart
flopped over
and lay still
while he passed(as

close as i'm to you
yes closer
made of nothing
except loneliness[25]

There is only one man.[26]

harness the sun, 1967
So: I see you – a very fresh, unique, wonderful individual. When I see you I can believe in lots of things: creativity, individuality, humanity, love, reciprocity – when I write, talk or think about you, clouds lift, light filters through and for a brief instant, I can see almost forever. And that's more than any human being such as I have a right to: and to have it so much, so often, makes me want to say grace all day long. Let no one speak of God's death – or nonexistence to me who have found him in this wondrous strange happening to out-

happen all happenings – our meeting. I believe in me through you – I believe in God through you.[27]

I feel good in a special way I'm in love and it's a sunny day.[28]

The world cannot be wrong If in this world there's you.[29]

How does it feel to be one of the beautiful people?[30]

things go better with, 1967
What men need today is faith in themselves and in others, release from the sense of their isolation and hope: a conviction that realities like justice, peace, unity and love, are not merely good things on paper, good things in songs, good things meant for the good alone. What men need is a reminder that these things are worth being born for…indeed that we were born for nothing else…[31]

with love to the everyday miracle, 1967
Conversion
is revolution
is growth
is living in a way
appropriate to
the coming age
and is not understood
by the present age
which is passing away
God descends, man ascends,
and they move on.[32]

yellow submarine, 1967
And our friends are all on board Many more of them live next door[33]

wet and wild, 1967
When he used this word "cup" he was talking about his cross…when he invited us to partake of his cup, he is not inviting us to take a little sip of grape juice, he is inviting us to participate in wall-breaking, in living and dying as a representative of God's shalom – reconciliation.[34]

jesus never fails, 1967
I get by with a little help from my friends[35]

come alive, 1967
The glory of Christ is man fully alive. Man fully alive is the glory of God.[36]

The blue cross way is very simple, we walk together.[37]

Don't you need somebody to love?[38]

that man loves, 1967
When God enters the world, he sets men in movement. Or rather, let us say, he gets with a movement already underway. He becomes a brother on the journey, so truly one of us as to know at bone and heart and marrow all the perplexity and pain, the darkness and setbacks and fits and starts of the human march. Later, much later, (and then only for a time), comes the single big word to burden our

faith: resurrection. The word is perhaps too large for men today to cope with. We say "yes" to it as best we can and turn again in our unrisen flesh and minds, to the unfinished business of living.[39]

Our personal life is as full of grief and private torment as a clown's is always said to be.[40]

let the sun shine, 1968
The creative revolution – to take a chunk of the imagined future and put it into the present – to follow the law of the future and live it in the present.[41]

news of the week, 1969
I am the hounded slave, I wince at the bite of the dogs,
Hell and despair are upon me, crack and again crack the marksmen,
I clutch the rails of the fence, my gore dribs, thinn'd with the ooze of my skin,
I fall on the weeds and stones,
The riders spur their unwilling horses, haul close,
Taunt my dizzy ears and beat me violently over the head with whip-stocks.

Agonies are one of my changes of garments,
I do not ask the wounded person how he feels, I myself become the wounded person,
My hurts turn livid upon me as I lean on a cane and observe.[42]

The plan of a slave ship, showing the conditions in which slaves crossed the Atlantic. The slave trade was abolished by Great Britain in 1807, and other countries were persuaded to follow suit in 1815.[43]

DEEPER INTO THE VIETNAM WAR: A Marine is evacuated during patrol action against the Vietcong.[44]

phil and dan, 1969
I recall what Thoreau said in his famous essay on civil disobedience, "under a government which imprisons unjustly, the true place for a just man is also in prison." To me therefore, prison is a very creative way to say yes to life and not to war.[45]

They were trying to make an outcry, an anguished outcry to reach the American community before it was too late. I think this is an element of free speech to try – when all else fails – to reach the community.[46]

if i, 1969
I challenge you today to see that his spirit never dies…and that we go forward from this time, which to me represents crucifixion on to a redemption and a resurrection of the spirit.[47]

He learns that the "yes" or "on" elements of energy cannot be experienced without contrast with the "no" or "off," and therefore that darkness and death are by no means the mere absence of light and life, but rather their origin. In this way the fear of death and nothingness is entirely overcome.

Because of this startling discovery, so alien to the normal common sense, he worships the divinity under its female form rather than its male form – for the female is symbolically representative of the negative, dark, and hollow aspect of the world, without which the masculine, positive, light, and solid aspect cannot be manifested or seen… he discovers that existence is basically a kind of dancing or music – an immensely complex energy pattern which needs no explanation other than itself – just as we do not ask what is the meaning of fugues…Energy itself, as William Blake said, is eternal delight – and all life is to be lived in the spirit of rapt absorption in an arabesque of rhythms…[In] Western Civilization… we over accentuate the positive, think of the negative as "bad," and thus live in a frantic terror of death and extinction which renders us incapable of "playing" life with a noble and joyous detachment. Failing to understand the musical quality of nature, which fulfils itself in an eternal present, we live for a tomorrow which never comes…. But through understanding the creative power of the female, of the negative, of empty space, and of death, we may at least become completely alive in the present.[48]

the cry that will be heard, 1969
Or put your girl to sleep sometime
With rats instead of nursery rhymes,
With hunger and your other children
By her side.
And wonder if you'll share your bed
With something else that must be fed,
For fear may lie beside you
Or it may sleep down the hall.

And it might begin to teach you
How to give a damn about your fellow man.

Come and see how well despair
Is seasoned by the stifling air
See your ghetto in the good old
Sizzling summertime.
Suppose the streets were all on fire,
The flames like tempers leaping higher,
Suppose you'd lived there all your life,
D' you think that you would mind?

And it might begin to reach you
Why I gave a damn about my fellow man,
And I might begin to teach you
How to give a damn about your fellow man.[49]

1
The compilation of these texts, which served as the basis for *Corita Reading,*
can be found in *Come Alive! The Sprited Art of Sister Corita,* Four Corners Books, London 2006.
2
Psalm 98.7–9.
3
Psalm 24.9.
4
Lyndon B. Johnson.
5
Samuel A. Eisenstein.
6
Sr. William (Helen Kelley) on Mary's Day 1964.
7
Langston Hughes, 'Dream Variations' from *The Collected Poems of Langston Hughes*, published by Alfred A. Knopf, a division of Random House, Inc.
8
Walt Whitman, *Song of Myself.*
9
Marcia Petty.
10
Unidentified author, US Pavilion, World's Fair.
11
Martin Luther King, Jr..
12
Albert Camus 'Create Dangerously' from *Resistance, Rebellion, and Death*, translated by Justin O'Brien, published by Alfred A. Knopf, a division of Random House, Inc.
13
Maurice Ouellet.
14
Daniel Berrigan.
15
Text by Maurice Ouellet, as quoted in *My People.*
16
Daniel Berrigan.
17
Gertrude Stein.
18
Gerald Huckaby, *I am in Vietnam.*
19
Daniel Berrigan.
20
Rainer Maria Rilke,'Letter Eight', *Letters To A Young Poet.*
21
Robert Frost, 'The Rose Family' taken from *The Poetry of Robert Frost* edited by Edward Connery Latham. Published by Jonathan Cape. Reprinted by permission of The Random House Group Limited.
22
Unidentified author.
23
Unidentified author.
24
Henry David Thoreau.
25
E. E. Cummings, 'no time ago', Copyright 1950, © 1978, 1991 by the Trustees for the E. E. Cummings Trust. Copyright © 1979 by George James Firmage, from *Complete Poems: 1904–1962* by E. E. Cummings, edited by George J. Firmage. Used by permission of Liveright Publishing Corporation.
26
Unidentified author.
27
Unidentified author.
28
John Lennon & Paul McCartney, *Good Day Sunshine.*
29
Charlie Chaplin, *This Is My Song.*
30
John Lennon & Paul McCartney, *Baby You're A Rich Man.*
31
Daniel Berrigan.
32
Unidentified author.
33
John Lennon & Paul McCartney, *Yellow Submarine.*
34
Unidentified author.
35
John Lennon & Paul McCartney, *With A Little Help From My Friends.*
36
Unidentified author.
37
Unidentified author.
38
Jefferson Airplane, *Don't You Want Somebody To Love?*
39
Daniel Berrigan.
40
Unidentified author.
41
Rabbi Arthur Waskow.
42
Walt Whitman, *Song Of Myself.*
43
Illustration caption.
44
Life magazine caption, 2 July 1965.
45
Thomas Lewis.
46
William Kunstler.
47
Coretta Scott King4.
48
Alan Watts, 'On the Tantra' from *Cloud-Hidden, Whereabouts Unknown* by Alan Watts (Copyright © Alan Watts). Reprinted by permission of A.M. Heath & Co Ltd.
49
Stuart Scharf and Robert Dorough, *Give A Damn* as recorded by Spanky & Our Gang / Mercury.

Tischreden (table speeches), 2013
Transcript of *Tischreden*
(table speeches), 2013, a
113-minute sound piece
featuring speeches by Franco
'Bifo' Berardi (read by Adrian
Williams), Liliane Weissberg,
Lise Soskolne/W.A.G.E., Carolyn
Christov-Bakargiev, and Claire
Pentecost on the topic of poverty.
The speeches were given on
1 March 2013 at a dinner held in
conjunction with the exhibition,
Andrea Büttner, at MMK Museum
für Moderne Kunst Frankfurt
am Main.

Franco 'Bifo' Berardi

Good evening, my name is Adrian
Williams, and I'm going to read the text
written for this evening by Franco
Berardi, who couldn't make it. So I hope
I do it justice. And I will follow that with
a poem that Andrea's asked me to select
that would be appropriate also for the
occasion of this lovely dinner.

Economic expansion is over and will
never come back.
Ungrowth is not a moral or political choice
that we can accept or refuse.
In Europe Ungrowth is a given, a conse-
quence of the redistribution of the world
division of labour and of the exhaustion
of physical resources.
If future is identified with economic
Growth, then the future is dead.
If richness is identified with having more
things to consume and more time to
work, then the future is dead.
Richness is enjoying time and sharing
what has already been produced,
fully deploying the productive force of
collective intelligence.
Call it poverty. It is a frugal way of being
happy with the richness that we have.
Richness and the good life have to be
disentangled from the capitalist expectation of never-ending Growth.
Financial dictatorship is reducing salaries
and increasing work-time and exploita-
tion, with the obvious result of growing
unemployment and spreading reces-
sion. But the reduction of work-time is
the only strategy that makes it possible
to transform Ungrowth into a process
of enrichment of the quality of life and of
collective pleasure.
A huge wave of protest has been spreading in the years 2010–2011, but the traditional forms of the movement's action
have exposed their ineffectiveness:
demonstrations, strikes, peaceful protests are ineffective because financial
power is based on disembodied dynamics, which are unattainable by the
physical bodies of the movement.
Only organized withdrawal, only massive
insolvency can defuse the financial
attack.
Refusal of paying the monetary and the
symbolic debt that is submitting our
lives to the financial dictatorship is the
way for emancipating social life from the
deadly dogma of debt.
Community currencies are proliferating
and will spread with the deepening of
the social disaster.
But in order to strengthen the process of
insolvency and autonomization, solidarity is needed, and solidarity can only
be based on empathy and the pleasure
of the presence of the body of the other.

For Andrea I've selected a poem
by Charles Bukowski published in 1979.
It's called 'The Red Porsche'

it feels good
to be driven about in a red
porsche
by a woman better-
read than I
am.
it feels good
to be driven about in a red
porsche
by a woman who can explain
things about
classical
music to
me.

it feels good
to be driven about in a red
porsche
by a woman who buys
things for my refrigerator
and my
kitchen:
cherries, plums, lettuce, celery,
green onions, brown onions,
eggs, muffins, long
chilis, brown sugar,
wine vinegar, pompeian olive oil
and red
radishes.

I like being driven about
in a red porsche
while I smoke cigarettes in
gentle languor.

I'm lucky. I've always been
lucky:
even when I was starving to death
the bands were playing for
me.
but the red porsche is very nice
and she is
too, and
I've learned to feel good when
I feel good.

it's better to be driven around in a
red porsche
than to own
one. the luck of the fool is
inviolate.

Liliane Weissberg

Ladies and Gentlemen:
Thank you so much for your attention.
Please continue with your meal; let me
just add a few words.
As I look around, and as I look at you,
I see men and women who are well
dressed. You are sitting at a table in a
leisurely fashion. You have been served
water, and even wine. You have food to
eat. In short, I can't really think of you
as poor. So this is actually a meal in
which we have to imagine what it would
mean to be poor, and how we could
confront poverty or counter poverty,
although my assumption is that poverty
is not part of our current experience.
And some of you may think, well: We feel
compassion for the poor, and we might
want to give the poor something, because we are charitable. We want to
help them: We want to give them money.
We want to give them goods. That is
very laudable, and we might say that it
comes from a Christian mind-set.

And then, you may think that poverty
is not only negative; perhaps it is also
something for which to strive. You
may want to get rid of worldly possessions, because worldly goods may
encumber your well-being. Those of you
who seek out poverty as a positive good
will reject material objects for the sake
of spiritual values. You may want to
concentrate on what is really important
to you, to seek independence from the
world of material pleasures, and even
to contemplate entering a cloister or
monastery – not that I think that many
people at this table have seriously been
thinking about that. But this idea that
poverty leads to a greater spirituality,
that by cleansing ourselves of the world
of material goods we may be closer to
God – this, too, is a very Christian idea.

So let me suggest what the difference is between a Jewish and a
Christian view on poverty. For Jews,
there is no material image of God. God
has no bodily extension. Is God, then,
devoid of a material being or physical
possessions, poor? Christians may
be able to say this about Jesus. But
neither Jews nor Christians will be able
to say this about God. Nobody has seen
God, and nobody can see God. Moses
went on the mountain to meet with God,
but Moses didn't see God, either. All he
saw was a tablet that he received, and
that contained the Ten Commandments.
Thus, we can say that Judaism is a
religion about an invisible God.

But Judaism is not just a religion;
it is a set of laws. Judaism is a legal
system, and a system offering social
guidelines, describing how Jews ought
to behave. And as such a system, it has
three very important pillars. First, Jews
are asked to believe in one, invisible
God. This is where law and religion
intersect. Secondly, they are asked to
study the Torah, the Holy Scripture, and
to learn. Perhaps it is in learning rather
than in the abandonment of worldly
goods that greater understanding can
be found, and hence a greater proximity
to God. Thirdly, however, Jews strive
for justice, a demand called "tzedakah."
This justice demands that we give,
and especially that we give for the poor.
Justice, however, is different from
compassion, and here is the difference
between the two attitudes towards
poverty that I mentioned before. I don't
want to imply that Jews do not feel

compassion for the poor, that they are unable to feel pity, that they lack charity. But Jewish giving should not be compelled by compassion, but by a sense of and for justice. By giving, you want to level out inequality. Giving is important as a step in the attempt to heal the world. Does that sound a little bit like the Occupy Movement? Yes, indeed it does.

So it is not compassion for the other person that guides your giving, but the demand that you be just person. What is the difference, you may ask? Well, the difference is twofold. First, I have to give to the poor not only because I encounter a poor individual, but because poverty itself is something that one should strive to eradicate. But most importantly, the focus is on the giver. It is in every person's interest to be giving and just. And this is precisely why every Jew is asked to give – whether he or she may be considered wealthy or poor – not just because wealth and poverty are relative, but because justice – tzedakah – is demanded from all.

This tzedakah was first and foremost a demand enacted for the members of a Jewish community and for Jewish institutions; everyone should be cared for. And thus, you are already able to see that poverty is not a positive in Judaism. The idea of gaining spirituality via the abdication of worldly goods is absent. Instead, Judaism supports the idea of balancing wealth, of healing through justice. And so, you give to other persons, and you give to Jewish institutions. And when you go to a synagogue, you will find even today little boxes that are called the tzedakah boxes, where people give funds to be distributed.

It has been thus for many generations. What is so interesting is that the demand to give has continued to be part of the Jewish tradition, even with Jews who no longer considered themselves religious or perhaps even Jewish at all. In the nineteenth century, when Jews entered bourgeois society, acculturated, even assimilated, they cared less about religious laws, but they still continued to give. Only the community had changed. They did not feel as close to their synagogues perhaps, or perhaps just as close to the new communities that they had entered: the village, the city, the state. When the German Reich was founded in 1871, Jews were emancipated, or rather: almost emancipated. Full emancipation came only after World War I; until 1918, Jews were not able to become university professors or army officers unless they converted. But gaining rights, they were eager to show their loyalty to the new state, to document their entry in this new society, and perhaps to offer some idea of justice here as well. Thus, a philanthropic tradition developed that transformed the giving for Jewish causes or to the Jewish poor to a giving for institutions not associated with Judaism at all. Jews became leading sponsors of public

hospitals, libraries, museum collections, or universities such as the one here in Frankfurt am Main.

Was this giving always done to advance justice? Or was there increasingly egoism as well? Was it always done to do good, or was it also done to be recognized and accepted? The medieval Jewish philosopher Moses Maimonides distinguished between eight kinds of giving in his definition of tzedakah, which is a very elaborate set of distinctions: eight kinds, not seven, and not nine. The first kind is the most egoistic one in which the person who receives the gift knows the giver, and hence has to thank him. It is much better, and a much higher form of giving, to give anonymously, to give without disclosing one's identity. But truly the highest form of giving is that by which you do not only help the poor on this or that occasion, but help the person (or institution) to become independent from future assistance, to encourage an equal standing between giver and recipient.

This is not the type of giving we most often encounter, of course. If you visit an American university – and I teach at one – you will see buildings that bear the names of donors, or family members of these donors. They have become memorials to those who are lost or would like to be remembered or simply admired. This is not anonymous giving, of course, and although many of these givers are Jewish or of Jewish descent, they do not follow the idea of tzedakah, as it was originally conceived. Perhaps it is just too easy to show wealth, a sign to us that justice is not yet in place.

Lise Soskolne / W.A.G.E.
W.A.G.E. stands for Working Artists and the Greater Economy. We're a group of visual and performance artists and independent curators fighting for the regulated payment of artist fees by the nonprofit art institutions who contract our labour.

So this is sort of a strange situation because Andrea and the museum have generously invited W.A.G.E. to share in this meal inside of this important museum to talk about poverty and economic inequity in the art world. W.A.G.E. is an activist group that addresses the role that not-for-profit art institutions play in preventing the artist's ability to survive within the greater economy by not paying us for our labour – so, W.A.G.E. may just indirectly bite the hand that is feeding us tonight. And in this context there might appear to be some contradiction in our claiming impoverishment in the face of so much affluence, especially when we participate in the creation of wealth, and we benefit from it too.

How can we complain? Artists have the privilege of getting to do what we want, when we want, and how we want. And sometimes we get to present our work in great cultural institutions like this, in a space like this, and like this exhibition which has been mounted with

such care and sensitivity that it affirms that what we make together – as artist and institution – has little to do with the creation of wealth. So it seems kind of inappropriate in such a place and at such a moment and in such company, to talk about *the fact that it has everything to do with the creation of wealth*, and that this wealth is unequally distributed. And that most of the time artists don't receive any form of compensation for their work, and that most of us – while being culturally affluent – live in relative material poverty. So it's exactly because this is the wrong moment and the wrong place to address it, that W.A.G.E. has been invited to speak here. And if I chose not to speak about inequity with candour tonight out of deference to the museum and the opportunity it has afforded me in being here, I'd be enacting the very relation that W.A.G.E. is working to overturn.

Demanding payment for services rendered and content provided is not an act of disrespect and there should be no shame in it. To bite the hand that feeds us because it's not feeding us what we deserve and need in order to live, and because it feeds us at its own arbitrary discretion, is really just to break with a relationship that is inequitable. Artistic labour supports a multi-billion dollar industry and yet – there are no standards, conventions or regulations for artist compensation. We sometimes receive artist fees if we ask for them, or they're dispensed at the discretion of the institution. As compensation for the work that we're asked to provide: preparation, installation, presentation, consultation, exhibition and reproduction, that sounds a lot like *charity to us*. And charity is a transaction.

But W.A.G.E. believes that charity is an inappropriate transaction within a robust art economy from which most get paid for their labour and others profit greatly, and we believe that the exposure we get from an exhibition does not constitute payment. We provide a work force. We refute the positioning of the artist as a speculator and call for the remuneration of cultural value in capital value.

We expect this from nonprofits precisely *because* they are nonprofit. They are granted special status because they serve the public good. This also means they're not subject to the laws of supply and demand for their survival. Instead they receive subsidies – charity, in fact – to do their work. A not-for-profit is by definition a public charity. A public charity also has a special moral status because it seems to operate outside of the commercial marketplace – it isn't subject to what profit demands from the rest of us. It doesn't have to compromise its ethics for the sake of capital. The white walls of the museum are also firewalls between integrity and capital, public good and profit margin, culture and compromise.

Paradoxically though, it is this very moral authority that imbues artworks and artists with economic value in the commercial marketplace. The logic is that if it's exhibited in a museum, it must have value beyond commerce – and it is exactly this perception which adds value to art when it reaches the commercial auction and sales markets. Moral authority also enables the nonprofit to raise money. The more of it it has, the more money it can raise. The more money it can raise, the more responsibility it has to compensate its employees and subcontractors equitably – both because it can afford to AND because it should.

The money that nonprofits receive from the state, private foundations and corporate sponsors is given to them with the contractual obligation that they will use it to present public exhibitions and programmes. That's what the money is given to them for. The nonprofit is a public charity but it is **not** a charity provider and artists are **not** a charity case because we earn our compensation – just like the director, the curator, and the graphic designer.

So, Artists: you also bear some responsibility in this equation. Don't tell yourself that you're lucky to be having an exhibition. You were subcontracted to produce content for an institution that receives charity for exactly that purpose. Exhibiting your work at an institution is a transaction. Even if 50,000 Euros are being spent to produce your artwork, those 50,000 Euros have been budgeted for, and an artist's fee should also be budgeted for separate from production costs, so that you can pay your bills, just like the salary of the person who wrote the budget, the salary of the person who did the fundraising – and even the person who donated the funds – they got a tax break. None of this is luck – it's a system.

Artists and arts administrators: we all need to change the way we think about this system because we are all responsible for it. That's what W.A.G.E. has been doing for the last five years.

If it's true that wages are often kept low in order to maximize profit, then there is a real opportunity here – since profit is not the goal – to set wages in terms of their real value, and in direct relation to the cost of living. This might mean making some changes to programmes and budgets. Let's imagine for a moment what that might look like.

What would it be like if artist fees were a distinct, separate, and visible line item in operating budgets? What would happen if instead of having 10 exhibitions per year and paying artist fees of $1,000 each to 20 artists, you presented 5 exhibitions and each artist got a $4,000 fee? Reducing production doesn't reduce profit at an art institution – slowing things down would just achieve greater equity.

What about an equation like this for paying artist fees: take the Director's salary of, for example, $100,000 and divide it by the number of exhibitions produced per year. $100,000 divided

by 5 exhibitions would mean that each artist would get a $20,000 fee for their work. An artist could almost live on $20,000 over the course of the year it took to prepare for the exhibition.

But we're going much further than that. We're using the artist fee as a starting point to think about *all* of the labour in an institution. For example, what would happen if the Director's salary were $50,000 instead of $100,000 and the security guard made $30,000 instead of $15,000? It's hard to imagine. And if the Director can't accept that kind of pay cut then more money should be raised because the biggest salary should not, and cannot, come at the expense of the compensation of those who are also fundamental to the organization's livelihood.

Institution, W.A.G.E. doesn't accept your claim of being a charity when you fundraise and a Capitalist when you design your budgets. W.A.G.E. challenges you to use your moral authority and special economic status to set new standards for the compensation of labour.

Institution, have we bitten your hand? Have we shamed you into understanding why we can no longer accept being written out of the economic equation? If so, maybe this was in fact the right place and the right moment to have done so. I'm pretty certain that not to have done so wouldn't have done justice to the very humble and radical proposition Andrea has made to us through her exhibition. Thank you Andrea.

Carolyn Christov-Bakargiev
Allora, I'm very lucky to be invited at the tail end of the dinner – so my stomach is full, and therefore my mind is loose and there's no blood there as it's all in the digestive system – invited by Andrea Büttner to share with you some ideas and thoughts about Arte Povera, which is indeed the subject through which Andrea and I met. Andrea came to Italy to do research about Arte Povera, and I happen to have written a lot about Arte Povera, especially twenty years ago, more or less. There were artists who were older than me, but who were not professors or teachers, and I remember learning a lot more from them than from university. And the tie with Bifo, with Franco Berardi, is interesting because although the Arte Povera artists were not friends with the Autonomia people, they were of the same period – a little bit earlier even. They were of the same generation as Mario Tronti, who was one of the inspirers of Autonomia who moved out of the Italian Communist party because he felt that the official Communists were just as much Productivists as the Capitalists, so he had the idea that one could withdraw from labour, withdraw from the system of production and distribution of what is produced in work, and this idea of strike or withdrawal – what Paolo Virno calls 'exodus'– was very much in Bifo's talk when he spoke. (And he doesn't

ride around in a Porsche with somebody that owns the Porsche; actually he lives very frugally in Bologna.) But it also explains the humus and the period of the 1960s and 1970s when the Arte Povera was in its so-called prime. Some of you know a later version of Arte Povera – the late works of artists sometimes become a little bit bigger and a little bit heavier to ship, it happens to the best of people. You know, we know also the late Picasso – some people like it, some people don't, and so on. Early Arte Povera, the beginning, the nurturing period of the Arte Povera, was a very important moment in European post World War II art, because it was a moment where suddenly it was possible that maybe we would not be lost thinking too much about consumer culture and thinking too much about reacting to consumer culture. Suddenly there were these pop artists winning prizes in the Venice Biennale and everyone needing to think about Marilyn Monroe, but why in the world should we think about Marilyn Monroe? Maybe we can think about coal, and maybe we can think about the processes of transforming a material according to the humidity and the temperature in the space. And maybe this business about consumer culture and spectacle will be remembered hundreds of years from now only as a small blip of a kind of regional style. [...]

Anyway, I could speak for hours, but I thought I might read you the beginning of a text. My relationship with Arte Povera goes all the way through friendships that still exist with Giuseppe Penone and others; through memories of people who are no longer with us like Alighiero Boetti, to whom, in dOCUMENTA (13), it was such a great privilege to pay homage by going with Mario Garcia Torres to Afghanistan and looking for the One Hotel and finding it and renting it, and Mario taking the bars off of the windows, planting roses, painting the outside and activating it again as a space of seminars; and Christoph Menke coming and doing a philosophy seminar; and the old garden of the old ex-hotel – the One Hotel – which was run as a real hotel by Alighiero Boetti when he was wearing a suit in half of his life, because the other half he was being an avant-grade hippy artist in Torino… But since I don't remember anything about Arte Povera, except for anecdotes and stories, which I could tell you for hours, I'm going instead to read something which I wrote twenty years ago or more or less [...]

I want to read you the quote of how Jean-Christophe Amman defined Arte Povera in 1970, since Susanne [Gaensheimer] said he was around the other day. In 1970 he offered a definition of Arte Poverta that is particularly relevant, he said: 'Arte Povera designates a kind of art which, in contrast with the technologized world around it, seeks to achieve a poetic statement with the simplest of means.' So povera – poor – in this case means simple, not only simple materials or simple means; also techniques like making a mono-chrome. So, there are moments of giving up authority in the making of the piece and the idea of co-making it.

And you wanted me to read one last thing…you wanted me to read the source for Celant. The source is Grotowski of course. Grotowski was one of the avant-garde theatre makers. He lived in Italy for a long time, he was Polish, and he wrote in 1965, which is ten years after television starts to be screened in Italy, and of course every-thing is in a competition to be more technological, quicker, faster – like today with wanting to have Quantum computers, so that you can have more money and so forth. He said that if you pare down, you also can be much more free. So he wrote in 1965: 'Theatre must admit its limits. If it cannot be richer than film, then let it be poorer. If it cannot be as lavish as television, then let it be ascetic. If it cannot create an attraction on a technical level, then let it give up all artificial technique. All that is then left is a "holy" actor in a poor theatre.' Which brings us to Grotowski's roots. Indeed, in this there might be medieval ideas of Christianity and poverty like St.Francis, which is something that Andrea has also been interested in, but I think it is important to open up. There are many, many other trajectories that also have a special relationship with so-called simplicity or humbleness, like Hinduism and Buddhism and even the ancient Greeks. We mustn't forget Diogenes and the beginning of the cynical school of philosophy. So, I guess it is about a kind of ecology of the mind and of matter and of welding together what Karen Barad would call today intra-action. That is all I have to say about Arte Povera.

Claire Pentecost
Okay. I think I am the last speech – I'm sorry, you're turning around. Where should I stand? Down here with Andrea.

I want to thank the museum for host-ing this event, and Bernd and Marijana for being in charge of the details on the ground. I want to thank Andrea for making a world for us, this beautiful exhibition, and I'd like to thank Kimberly because she's very creative without being contrived, and she makes good tasting food.

Okay, what I'm thinking about is the materialization of the sign. So, if my remarks had a title, that would be the title, 'The Materialization of the Sign', to bring the sign into the realm of the material. I'm going to tell this in a story, a vision, a poem and a menu. Those are the forms. And so we begin.

A story
Food, in some places, some very influ-ential places, has ceased to be food. It has become numbers. It has become numbers that signify prices. This is the ultimate reduction, the most impov-erished abstraction, where you think

of a thing that people have enjoyed and shared and produced as long as human-ity has been around, and see that thing reduced to numbers, to prices. This is a form of impoverishment. This is because food is now an investment. Somewhere around 1991 the firm of Goldman Sachs created an index fund that offered inves-tors the chance to make money off of food. Before this time there were regula-tions to keep people from speculating on food, because everyone needs food. Food is not an option. But Goldman Sachs was very persuasive, and they persuaded the regulators to ease these restrictions, and they created an index fund that's much more complicated than I can relate to you now. But it meant that people with money, who have nothing to do with food or farming, could invest their money and make more money. People with money want to make money off of the money they already have, right? That's how our system works. It's interesting because governments have an interest in keeping food at a price that's within everyone's reach, because food and revolution are historically related.

[…] The economic crash of 2008, which continues today, was experienced in many parts of the world as a food crisis. The weird thing about 2008 was that the world produced more grains than ever, and yet hunger rose to un-precedented levels. So what happened was that there was plenty of food, but there were hunger riots in record numbers, and maybe the people in affluent countries weren't paying atten-tion, but that was one of the major characteristics of 2008. Because of the speculation on food as commodity the prices rose, and people couldn't afford to buy the food. We had lots of food, but people couldn't afford it. In fact, many people have said that this was a major contribution to the background that determined the timing of what is known as the Arab Spring. Egypt was just one of the countries where the price of bread was out of people's reach and there were food riots. So the conversion of food to a set of numbers, a price, a financially rendered abstraction, made food – the real thing that we use to sustain our lives – it made it inac-cessible to real people, with real stom-achs, but no real money.

I'm just throwing around this concept of the real and assuming you know what I mean, even though for centuries, since Socrates and Plato, our culture has ques-tioned what is real and millions of gal-lons of ink have been spilled on this topic, but I will just assume we all know what I'm talking about, the things that are not abstracted into numbers and prices.

The ongoing economic crisis that began in 2008 has made many people uncertain of where to put their money. As none of the usual investments seem safe anymore, the people with money started to invest in food and in land to grow food. 2008 also marks the stag-

gering acceleration of the phenomenon known as land grabbing, which is just what it sounds like: people with money and governments with money, espe-cially those worried about feeding their people in the coming uncertain times of environmental chaos, are investing in farmland. Mostly, but not exclusively, in the countries that have less money, in Africa, South America, parts of Asia and so forth. Investment funds, hedge funds, pension funds, sovereign wealth funds, venture capitalists are obtaining long leases, 50–100 years, on huge tracts of land in countries largely popu-lated by subsistence farmers. The prob-lem is that these farmers are being evicted from their lands in order to make way for the new investment, which is billed as progress. […] Things like palm oil, sugar cane, bio fuels and animal feed are being grown on these rented tracts of land. They're being grown for export, for cash. These crops will not feed the people who've been forcibly removed from the land they've farmed for generations. These crops are signi-ficant now as numbers in a global market system.

A Vision
[…] Whenever we eat, we consume both signs and real material food. In real life they're inseparable. Clearly the financial markets are not the only place where real things rise into the ether of signification. All of us as humans have the capacity for metaphor. The vigor-ous creativity of language is founded on metaphor. The miracle of our linguistic capacity is that really existing things are experienced simultaneously as signs in our imagination and materials knowable through our bodies.

So in confronting this complicated project, I did what I always do: I did a lot of research. Among other things, this included looking at memorable meals from history, especially art history. And I was reminded of the artist Gordon Matta-Clark's famous 'bone dinner' that he staged at the restaurant he founded with many other artists in Soho in 1971 called, quite simply, Food. Matta-Clark's best known work involved creating absences in buildings that were slated for demolition. He both took from the buildings and enriched them to make them sculpture, and I thought this was a really interesting gesture – that you can both take something away and enrich at the same time. The fabulous Chinese American activist Grace Lee Boggs who lives in Detroit says that the com-ing revolution is the first revolution in which we have to ask for less, not more, because as Bifo's text so eloquently explained, we have to redefine the good life as involving less material gains.

Okay so we have bones. I had bones from Matta-Clark's work. I wanted to commemorate him by including bones on this menu. Then, some weeks ago with the menu on my mind, I woke one morning with a small vision, a fragment, a remnant maybe of a dream. It was the image of a heart wrapped in a fist. Somehow I decided this would be the signal node of the menu. So now I'm thinking of bone and heart, things very material in living bodies, but also things with a long history of metaphoric value. Heart, bone. Bone, heart. The rag and bone shop of the heart. 'The foul rag and bone shop of the heart' is the last line of W. B. Yeats' poem 'The Circus Animals' Desertion'. This line became the *ritornelle*, or refrain, the menu was singing to me.

A Poem
The Irish poet William Butler Yeats, a late Romanticist and early Modernist, wrote 'The Circus Animals' Desertion' when he was 70 years old, very near the year of his death in 1939. The poem begins:

I sought a theme and sought for it in vain,

Here's the poet who's looking for ideas for a new poem, but finding nothing. In the absence of new ideas, he reviews his brilliant fifty year career with a very harsh eye. He writes:

Winter and summer till old age began
My circus animals were all on show,
Those stilted boys, that burnished chariot
Lion and woman and the Lord knows what.

What can I but enumerate old themes,

And for the next three verses, he does just that. He enumerates the major themes of the celebrated poems of William Butler Yeats, and he calls them circus animals, creatures enslaved for spectacle. And he sums it all up very regretfully writing:

Players and painted stage took all my love,
And not those things that they were emblems of.

It seems the poet fears he has wasted his life confusing images, or signs, and imagination with the real, wondering now that his circus animals have deserted him, if he placed his love in illusions. Then he softens a little and writes:

Those masterful images because complete
Grew in pure mind, but out of what began?

Here he concedes that his images were in fact masterful, and that he conceived them with the best intentions, but tuning himself now to the real within the noise of illusion, he questions what those images were actually made of, and what does he find? And I quote:

A mound of refuse or the sweepings of a street,
Old kettles, old bottles, and a broken can,
Old iron, old bones, old rags, that raving slut

Who keeps the till. Now that my ladder's gone,
I must lie down where all ladders start
In the foul rag and bone shop of the heart.

It's a beautiful and by now very famous and overused last line. In the foul rag and bone shop of the heart. But what is a rag and bone shop? It is a beautiful metaphor given life by the poet, but following the poet's own new feeling for the real, we acknowledge that it was also a really existing nineteenth-century and early-twentieth-century institution. So we come to the image of the rag picker. Who was the rag picker? We've seen Manet's painting of a rag picker; Atget's many photographs of rag pickers and their huts. Baudelaire also availed himself of this figure in a poem dedicated to wine. Among the poorest of the poor were men, women and children who picked through the rubbish of the city looking for any material that might be useful to someone, worth some pennies. Among the old kettles, old bottles, broken cans, iron scraps, they also looked for bones and rags. Bone and rag shops made paper from these materials. Rags for the fiber, and bones for the glue binder. Paper is the material of the poet. So where Yeats must go lie down in order to find a start of a new poetic ladder, it's not just a moving metaphor, it's a real place, a real material, the substrate of his craft made of the pickings of garbage.

A Menu
Now we're really almost done. To become real food, the image of a heart closed in a fist was transformed into a beet root enclosed in salt crust, a crust that had to be broken to free the heart, a process we thought would be most appropriate as a shared activity, hence the sharing of the first dish. The heart of a winter root vegetable became an animal heart in the next course. A real heart, not a metaphor, but still a metaphor, because all hearts are metaphors. Here it is the heart of a calf in a bed of winter greens, eaten in small portions because very precious. The next course is made of rags – the fibrous foods, pumpkin and kohlrabi. Rags to make paper? No, rags to make poo to mix with straw and return to the ground to nourish the next season of growing. You will notice the bronzes that adorn the tables. They are casts commissioned by Andrea of zebra poo and straw. This dish is not afraid to borrow that motif. And at last we get to the bones. For the main course we served you bones from which we picked the heart, the marrow out, and then we filled it with maybe a poorer protein. We discussed this whole marrow bone thing for a while, because Andrea was concerned that now because of the St. John's restaurant in London, marrow bones are the treat of posh boys and art students, so in case you rejected that tidbit, maybe you know now that it's

actually very posh – served with beans and potatoes, foods that have kept multitudes alive for millennia.

What you still have coming is dessert, and for dessert we borrowed a game from the Swiss artist Daniel Spoerri. A game of rich and poor determined by chance. For the rich, *pain perdu*, leftover bread made into a pudding with nuts and caramel, served with cardamom ice cream. You with the red slips are the rich. For you with the blue, a Mexican treat, a tortilla with butter and cinnamon sugar. You're welcome to share. Then there'll be one last plate, an exotic surprise that used to be the ultimate treat, once a year, that here is grounded in the real. And a liquor of which I forgot the name. So enjoy the last two courses, and thank you so much for being so game, so sporting, as to eat what's put in front of you.

Malin with Clay, 2007, screen print, 120 × 160 cm

Biography

Andrea Büttner
1972 born in Stuttgart
Lives and works in London and Frankfurt am Main

2010
PhD, Royal College of Art, London, UK

2003
Magister, Art History and Philosophy, Humboldt
University Berlin, Berlin, Germany

2000
Meisterschülerin, Berlin University of the Arts, Berlin,
Germany

Since 2012
Professor at Kunsthochschule Mainz, Mainz, Germany

Selected solo exhibitions:

2013
Andrea Büttner, Milton Keynes Gallery, Milton Keynes,
UK
Andrea Büttner, MMK Museum für Moderne Kunst,
Zollamt, Frankfurt am Main, Germany

2012
Andrea Büttner, International Project Space,
Birmingham, UK
Moos/Moss, Hollybush Gardens, London, UK

2011
The Poverty of Riches, Whitechapel Gallery, London,
UK/Collezione Maramotti, Reggio Emilia, Italy
Three New Works, Artpace, San Antonio, USA
Our Colours are the Colours of the Marketplace,
Art Statements, Art Basel (with Hollybush Gardens,
London), Basel, Switzerland

2009
Andrea Büttner, Croy Nielsen, Berlin, Germany

2008
Nought to Sixty – Andrea Büttner, Institute of
Contemporary Arts, London, UK
*It's so wonderful to be a woman and an artist in the
21st century*, Crystal Palace, Stockholm, Sweden
Andrea Büttner, Hollybush Gardens, London, UK

2007
On the spot #1 – Andrea Büttner, Badischer
Kunstverein, Karlsruhe, Germany

Selected group exhibitions:

2013
Andrea Büttner / Joëlle de la Casinière / Gareth Moore,
Catriona Jeffries, Vancouver, Canada
The Assistants, David Kordansky Gallery, Los Angeles,
USA

2012
Documenta 13, Kassel, Germany
Documenta 13, Kabul, Afghanistan
Soundworks, Institute of Contemporary Arts, London,
UK
Brannon, Büttner, Kierulf, Kierulf, Kilpper, Bergen
Kunsthall, Bergen, Norway
Reversibility, curated by Pierre Bal-Blanc,
Peep-Hole, Milan, Italy

2011
When is a Human Being a Woman?, Hollybush Gardens,
London, UK
*Independent Curators International presents FAX and
Project 35*, South London Gallery, London, UK
Heimatkunde: 30 Künstler blicken auf Deutschland,
Jewish Museum Berlin, Berlin, Germany
If It's Part Broke, Half Fix It, Contemporary Art Centre,
Vilnius, Lithuania
Qui admirez-vous?, La Box, Bourges, France

2010
An Affirmative Attitude, Hollybush Gardens, London,
UK
There is Always a Cup of Sea to Sail in, 29th São Paulo
Biennial, São Paulo, Brazil
Unto this Last, Raven Row, London, UK
Les compétences invisibles 1/3, Maison Populaire,
Centre d'art Mira Phalaina, Montreuil, France

2009
*The young people visiting our ruins see nothing but
a style* (curated by Form Content, London),
GAM Galleria Civica D'Arte Moderna e Contemporanea,
Turin, Italy
East International (selected by Art & Language and
Raster), Norwich, UK

2008
No one needs the needy, Galerie Sandra Buergel,
Berlin, Germany
Reversibility, The Fair Gallery (a project by Hollybush
Gardens, GB Agency, Jan Mot, Raster; curated by
Pierre Bal-Blanc, CAC Bretigny), Frieze Art Fair,
London, UK
Soft Shields of Pleasure, Den Frie Udstillingsbygning,
Copenhagen, Denmark
Raster: L'artista nella rinunicia 2: Transfert, Instituto
Polacco di Roma, Rome, Italy
Artist in Resignation, Raster, Warsaw, Poland

2007
Overtake – The Reinterpretation of Modern Art, Lewis
Glucksman Gallery, Cork, Ireland
Pensée sauvage – On Freedom, Frankfurter
Kunstverein, Frankfurt am Main, Germany/
Ursula BlickleStiftung, Kraichtal, Germany
Species of Spaces and Other Pieces, Hollybush
Gardens, London, UK
Evangelisch Katholisch VII Finale, Montgomery, Berlin,
Germany

2006
Anxiety of Influence, New Wight Biennial,
UCLA, Los Angeles, USA

Bloomberg New Contemporaries, Coach Shed, Liverpool, UK/Club Row, London, UK
Happy Believers, 7. Werkleitz Biennale, Halle, Germany

2005
Arbeiten auf Papier, Villa Grisebach Gallery, Berlin, Germany
Research in Progress, Cafe Gallery Projects, London, UK

2004
In erster Linie – 21 Künstlerinnen und das Medium Zeichnung, Kunsthalle Fridericianum, Kassel, Germany

Stipends/Awards:

2012
1822-Kunstpreis, Frankfurt am Main, Germany

2011
Artpace, San Antonio, USA

2010
Max Mara Art Prize for Women in collaboration with the Whitechapel Gallery, London, UK
American Academy, Rome, Italy

2009
Maria Sibylla Merian-Preis, Ministerium für Wissenschaft und Kunst, Hessen, Germany

2005
British Institution Award, London, UK

Bibliography

Artist's writing:

Andrea Büttner and Isla Leaver-Yap, 'Re: Andacht zum kleinen', *The Assistants*, Fionn Meade, ed., Mousse Publishing, Milan, 2013.

Andrea Büttner, 'Ideal Syllabus: Andrea Büttner', *Frieze*, Issue 152, Jan/Feb 2013.

Andrea Büttner, 'Of this I would have been shy not a year ago' in *Dieter Roth: Diaries*, Fiona Bradley, ed., Yale University Press, New Haven, 2012.

Andrea Büttner, 'Inverted Interview # 3' (with Lars Bang Larsen), *The Responsive Subject: From OOOOOO to FFFFFF*, FormContent, London, 2011.

Andrea Büttner, 'Now I am Somebody' in *Dieter Roth/Björn Roth, Worktables and Tischmatten*, Barry Rosen, ed., Yale University Press, New Haven, 2010.

Andrea Büttner, 'Inverted Interview # 1' (with Ben Borthwick), *Soft Shields of Pleasure*, Space Poetry, Copenhagen, 2008.

Andrea Büttner, 'Do something that is easy to do', *Material*, Issue 1, Los Angeles, 2008.

Andrea Büttner, 'Scham – Jedes Wort ist eine Blamage', *Sinn-haft*, Vienna, 2005.

Selected Bibliography:

Sylvia Staude, 'Minerva an der Supermarktkasse', *Frankfurter Rundschau*, 18 February 2013.

Michael Hierholzer, 'Tafel mit kargem Schmuck. Kartoffeln, Steine, Zebrakot: Arbeiten von Andrea Büttner im MMK Zollamt', *Frankfurter Allgemeine Zeitung*, 2 February 2013, No. 40.

Carolyn Christov-Bakargiev, Eva Scharrer, et al., *dOCUMENTA (13), Das Begleitbuch/The Guidebook*, catalogue volume 3/3. Hatje Cantz Verlag, Osfildern, Germany, 2012.

Steinar Sekkingstad and Solveig Øvstebø, eds., *Matthew Brannon, Andrea Büttner, Annette Kierulf, Caroline Kierulf, Thomas Kilpper*, catalogue, with texts by Solveig Øvstebø, Steinar Sekkingstad, and Lars Bang Larsen, Bergen Kunsthall, Bergen, Norway, 2012.

Fionn Meade, 'Reenchanted, Object-Oriented', *Spike Art Quarterly*, No. 33, Autumn 2012.

'Watchlist: Künstlerin des Monats: Andrea Büttner', *Monopol*, August 2012.

Konstanze Crüwell, 'Bescheidenes Glück im Vergnügungspark', *Frankfurter Allgemeine Sonntagszeitung*, 1 July 2012, No. 26, p. R5.

Charlotte Bonham-Carter, 'Andrea Büttner', *Art in America*, May 2012.

Laura McLean-Ferris, 'Andrea Büttner's "Moos/Moss", Hollybush Gardens, London', *Art-Agenda*, 16 February 2012.

Garden, 2008, screen print, 120 × 160 cm

Whitechapel Gallery, *Andrea Büttner: The Poverty of Riches*, with text and interview by Bina von Stauffenberg, Whitechapel Gallery, London, 2011.

Jewish Museum Berlin, *Heimatkunde: 30 Künstler blicken auf Deutschland*, catalogue, with texts by Inka Bertz, Margret Kampmeyer-Käding, Cilly Kugelmann, Martina Lüdicke und Mirjam Wenzel, Hirmer Verlag, Munich, 2011.

Laura Barnett, 'Andrea Büttner: the habit of art', *The Guardian*, 14 March 2011.

Lars Bang Larsen, 'Looking Back Looking Forward', *Frieze*, Issue 136, Jan/Feb 2011.

Alice Motard, *Unto the Last*, Raven Row, London, 2010.

Agnaldo Farias, Moacir dos Anjos, Chus Martinez, et al., Catalogue of the 29th Bienal de *São Paulo : there is always a cup of sea to sail in*, Fundaçao Bienal de São Paulo, Sao Paulo, 2010.

Martin Herbert, 'Focus: Andrea Büttner. Camcorders, convents, collectivism and confession', *Frieze*, Issue 133, September 2010, pp. 118–9.

Richard Birkett, 'Andrea Büttner', *MAP Magazine*, Issue # 23, Autumn 2010, pp. 44–9.

'Andrea Büttner: Artists at Work', *Afterall*, http://www.afterall.org/, 25 May 2010.

Anja Casser / Badischer Kunstverein, eds., *Andrea Büttner: I believe every word you say*, catalogue, Badischer Kunstverein, argobooks, Berlin, 2009.

Ian Kiaer, 'Top 10', *Artforum*, September 2009.

ICA, *Nought to Sixty*, catalogue, Institute of Contemporary Arts, London, 2008.

Chus Martinez, 'Andrea Büttner', *Artforum*, Best of 2008, December 2008.

'Artists Dictionary – Focus London', *Flash Art*, No. 262, October 2008.

Rajesh Punj, 'Andrea Büttner', *Art Review*, Issue 23, London, June 2008.

Michael Hübl, 'Was heisst eigentlich Scham? Badischer Kunstverein startet mit Andrea Büttner neue Ausstellungsreihe', *Badische Neue Nachrichten*, 28 Sept 2007.

'Pensée sauvage – Von Freiheit', *Frankfurter Kunstverein/Revolver*, Frankfurt, 2007.

Les Formes du délai, catalogue, La Box Bourges, 2007.

Anxiety of Influence, catalogue, *The New Wight Biennial*, UCLA, Los Angeles, 2006.

Bloomberg New Contemporaries 2006, catalogue, London, 2006.

Happy Believers, catalogue, *7 Werkleitz Biennale*, Halle, 2006.

In erster Linie – 21 Künstlerinnen und das Medium Zeichnung, catalogue, Kunsthalle Fridericianum, Kassel, 2004.

Michael Angele, 'Rührend leben und kämpfen', *Frankfurter Allgemeine Zeitung*, 16 October 2001, Berliner Seiten.

Author Biographies

Lars Bang Larsen is an independent curator, writer and art historian who completed his PhD at the University of Copenhagen on the subject of psychedelic concepts in neo-avant-garde art. He has curated numerous group exhibitions including *The Society Without Qualities*, Tensta Konsthall, Stockholm (2013), and *A History of Irritated Material*, Raven Row, London (2010). His books include *The Model: A Model for a Qualitative Society 1968* (2010) and *The Critical Mass of Mediation* (with Søren Andreasen, 2012).

Richard Birkett has been Curator of Artists Space, New York since 2010. He studied Fine Art at the Slade School of Fine Art and Goldsmiths College before running the non-profit gallery, Whitechapel Project Space, for six years and was curator at the Institute of Contemporary Arts in London (2007–2010).

Chus Martinez has been Chief Curator at El Museo del Barrio, New York since 2013. Her curatorial credits include *Documenta 13* (2012) the *Bienal de São Paulo* (2010) and the Cyprus Pavilion at the *Venice Biennale* (2005). She was Chief Curator at the Museu d'Art Contemporani de Barcelona (2008–2010), Director of the Frankfurter Kunstverein (2005–2008) and the Artistic Director of Bilbao's Sala Rekalde contemporary art space (2002–2005).

Hans-Ulrich Obrist is Co-Director of Exhibitions and Programmes and Director of International Projects at the Serpentine Gallery, London. Prior to this he was Curator of the Musée d'Art Moderne de la Ville de Paris (2000–2006), as well as curator of museum in progress, Vienna (1993–2000). Other projects include *Cities on the Move* (1996-1999), the 1st *Berlin Biennale* (1998), *Laboratorium* (1999), *Dakar Biennale* (2004), 1st & 2nd Moscow Biennale (2005 and 2007) and *Do It* (1993-2013). His publications include *A Brief History of Curating* (2008), *Cedric Price, Conversations*, (2010), *Interviews* Volumes 1 and 2 (2003 and 2010).

Nikolaus Hirsch is the Dean of the Städelschule and Director of Portikus, Frankfurt. His architectural work includes such award-winning projects as the Dresden Synagogue, Hinzert Document Center, Bockenheimer Depot Theater (with William Forsythe), Unitednationsplaza (with Anton Vidokle), European Kunsthalle and Cybermohalla Hub in Delhi. He curated *ErsatzStadt: Representations of the Urban*, Volksbühne, Berlin (2005), *Cultural Agencies* in Istanbul (2009), numerous exhibitions at Portikus and was recently appointed as director of the upcoming Gwangju Folly project in Korea.

List of works in exhibition at MMK

Tischreden (table speeches), 2013
Sound installation, 113 minutes

Tische (tables), 2013
Installation with 13 tables, 13 sheets of glass,
13 tablecloths, 27 grape juice bottles, various pictorial
and written material, parcel twine

Benches (stack), 2011/2013
Wood, plastic crates

Tischschmuck (table decorations), 2013
Cast bronze, multiple pieces

Breadpebble, 2010
Woodcut

Tent (marquee), 2012
Woodcut, diptych

Fabric Paintings, 2013
Stretched fabric

Minerva, 2011
Video, 5:39 minutes

Loans:

Kurt Schwitters
Untitled (cast of a pebble sculpture),
1944/47, 1956
Painted plaster, Cast Ex. 6/7
Kurt and Ernst Schwitters Foundation
Sprengel-Museum Hannover

Salvador Dalí
Christ on a Pebble, 1959
Oil on stone, Galerie Taimei, Japan

Georges Hugnet
Painted Stone in Form of a Mask, 1955
Oil on stone, Martin du Louvre, Paris

Stone from the Fels Cave, ca. 15,000 years old, found
in 1998
2 Stones from the Fels Cave, ca. 15,000 years old,
found in 2010
Painted limestones
Archaeological State Museum of Baden-Württemberg
and the Department of Early Prehistory at Eberhard
Karls University of Tübingen

List of works in exhibition at MK Gallery

Little Sisters: Lunapark Ostia, 2012
HD video, 42 minutes

Benches, 2011/2013
Wood, plastic crates, handwoven fabric

Untitled (bronze shelf), 2012
Cast bronze

Untitled (cardboard object on bronze shelf), 2012
Cardboard house won at Lunapark Ostia and cast
bronze shelf

Tische (tables), 2013
Installation with 4 tables, 4 sheets of glass, 4 tablecloths, various pictorial and written material

Tischreden (table speeches), 2013
Sound installation, 113 minutes

Tischschmuck (table decorations), 2013
Cast bronze, multiple pieces

Grid, 2012
Woodcut

Corner, 2011
Woodcut

Corner, 2011
Woodcut

Tent (two colours), 2012
Woodcut

Tent (marquee), 2012
Woodcut, diptych

Tent (pink), 2010
Woodcut

Untitled (three kings), 2012
Woodcut

Dancing Nuns, 2007
Woodcut

Dancing Nuns, 2007
Woodcut

Grille, 2007
Woodcut

Grille, 2006
Screen print

*HAP Grieshaber / Franz Fühmann: Engel der
Geschichte 25: Engel der Behinderten, Classen Verlag
Düsseldorf 1982, (HAP Grieshaber / Franz Fühmann:
Angel of History 25: Angel of the Disabled)*, 2010
Xerox and clip frames

Kabul Portfolio, 2012
20 woodcuts

Fabric Paintings, 2013
Stretched fabric

Fish, 2008, screen print, 120 × 160 cm

MUSEUM FÜR MODERNE KUNST
FRANKFURT AM MAIN

JÜRGEN PONTO-STIFTUNG
zur Förderung junger Künstler
1977 gegründet von Ignes Ponto und der Dresdner Bank

KULTURAMT
STADT FRANKFURT AM MAIN

FREUNDE DES MMK

Ramp, 2010, screen print, 120 × 160 cm